LEFT IN PEACE NOT PIECES

LEFT IN PEACE NOT PIECES

Pain Power Purpose,
The SIMBA way

Ousha Demello

ISBN: 978-1-7399431-1-0

The strategies in this book are presented primarily for enjoyment and educational purposes. The information and resources provided in this book are based upon the author's personal experience and professional expertise. Any outcome is based on the author's experience and there is no guarantee that your experience will be the same or that you will have similar results.

Although the author and publisher have made every effort to ensure that the information in this book was correct at press time, the author and publisher do not assume and hereby disclaim any liability to any party for any personal or professional loss, damage or disruption caused by errors or omissions, whether such errors or omissions result from negligence, accident, or any other cause.

Edited by: Caroline Bracey
Cover Designed by: Rose Miller
Book Interior design by: Richaa Sowambar
Book Critic: Dr. Francis Ikhenemoh
Publisher: Addea Media

The Author reserves the right to make changes at any time.

Acknowledgements

My wholehearted gratitude to my husband Peter Demello, my rock, best friend, and biggest fan.

Dheemyantee Kissoon, my beautiful mum, for her strength, keeping me safe, for her love, care, bravery, and good-heartedness.

My brothers Vinay, Vikash, and Vimal Kissoon, my sisters Savita Daboo, Indra Sowambar, and Devianee Espitia for their unconditional love and for stepping up to also parenting me. I am forever grateful to my family Sheela, Mahen, Lovena Somauroo, Kavita Gilchrist, Devika Kissoon for their love and support. Thank you to all Kissoon family especially my cousin Ravin, Yogeeta, and Hema for taking care of me during the most challenging time of my life.

To my in-laws, Jan Demello, Francis Demello, Jim Harford, Kelly Demello, Fatima Gomes, and Angela Gomes for loving me as their own daughter, sister and for always supporting me.

Thank you to my friend Kavish Mahadeo who helped, and supported me through the difficult journey and encouraged me to take the right action, and to all my beautiful girlfriends, for always being there for me.

I would also like to thank the Business, Computing and Travel team at Westherts college Joanne, Nadia, Karen, Florence, Dupe, Caroline C, Paul, Etse, for their love and support and a massive thank you to Theresa Simmons for her love, advice, and support. And special thanks to John Opolot, who supported me in the journey and, Caroline Bracey for editing my book.

I am eternally grateful to Jessen James Chinnapan who has helped me find my purpose and taught me how to share my story in order to serve and inspire others, and Chloe Bisson, who inspires me every time I hear her speak. To my dear friend Dr. Francis Ikhenemoh for his love, trust, and friendship, and gave me the title of this book.

My sincere gratitude to Dea Fileva for going the extra mile to help and guide me step by step to further edit and publish this book.

To all the amazing mentors and members of Professional Speaker School, Entrepreneurs Business Academy, and Queen in Business (Chloe, Tanya, Carrie, Shim, Marjah & Sunna), all the Billion lives changed team and ambassadors (Ikhenemoh, Harj, Sandra, Jessica, Tharan, John, Julie & Henna) for the ripple effect of helping and inspiring others.

To everyone who reads and believes in this book, I hope this book encourages and inspires you to embark on the immensely fulfilling challenge of life and trust that this gives you the courage and freedom to achieve a fulfilled life.

Dedication

This book is dedicated to all the men and women worldwide who have been made to feel that their life has no worth, felt intimidated, isolated, told they were good for nothing and thought they had to change themselves to fit in. There may be many reasons to bring you down, but you can find just the one reason to get you back up again.

Nothing lasts forever, not even pain!

To those with a story similar to mine but who do not have a voice to share them.

YOU ARE NOT ALONE!

> "You are not being buried, you are being planted."
>
> Christine Cane

Contents

Introduction

"You never know
how strong you are...
until being strong is
the only option you
have."

Cayla Mills

The sad truth

Domestic abuse is not always physical. The official government definition recognises different types of abuse, including physical, emotional, and financial. When it comes to domestic violence, people think of the stereotypes that go along with it. The truth is that domestic abuse can happen to anyone, no matter your age, gender, religion, ethnicity, educational level, or profession. Some forms of abuse are coercive control, an act or a pattern of acts of assault, isolation from family and support, threats, humiliation, and intimidation, depriving them of independence, or other abuse used to harm, punish, and exploit or frighten their victim.

Some common examples of coercive behaviour are:

- Monitoring and controlling your time
- Isolating you from friends and family
- Depriving you of basic needs, such as food and comfort
- Monitoring you via online communication tools or spyware
- Taking control over aspects of your everyday life, such as where you can go, who you associate with what you can wear and when you can sleep
- Depriving you access to support services, such as medical services
- Repeatedly putting you down, such as saying you're worthless and calling you names
- Humiliating, degrading, or dehumanising you
- Controlling your finances
- Making threats or intimidating you

- Exert power and control over a person through fear

The sad truth is that nearly two million people in the UK suffer some form of domestic abuse each year. One in four women and one in six men have been affected by domestic abuse in their lifetime, leading to an average of two women being murdered each week and thirty men per year.

Astonishingly, on average, there will have been thirty assaults before a victim calls the police, and victims ask for help from professionals an average of five times before receiving practical support to stop the abuse.

Research has shown that although men and women both suffer domestic abuse, the abuse suffered by women is more physically severe. It is likely to go on for longer and is more likely to result in them being injured or hospitalised. Both male and female victims are more likely to be disabled, from black or ethnic minority groups, or Low-income groups.

I am not a psychiatrist,
a social worker,
or a domestic abuse
specialist.

I am simply one woman
sharing my story and
strategies to overcome
my problems.

Unfortunately, I also
formed part of the
statistics above.

The yellow line

"One decision can make or break your life."

Quora

Have you ever been at a crossroad in your life and you are not quite sure what to do next?

June the 4th, 2010, was a beautiful sunny Friday. I was excited to be able to leave the house to go to work. As I settled down to start work at 9 AM, I was informed that I needed to meet with Dr. Jones, the Director of the college, in 15 minutes. I did not know what it was about, but I was excited as I had been working so hard lately and went the extra mile to produce soaring quality work at constricting deadlines.

It was swamped at the college lately as there were a lot of changes in the higher education industry, so we had to stay and work extra hours. I thought 'a pay rise perhaps or a promotion'. In the worst case, I was confident that the least I would probably get would be praise and appreciation for my hard work.

I looked at the clock, and it was nearly 15 minutes past, so I made my way to Dr. Jones' office.

He was not there, so I went in and sat on a brown leather chair near his desk. The chair was downy compared to the one we have in the office. I could hear everyone rushing around outside his office, but his office was hushed.

As I sat down quietly and looked at all his certificates hanging on his wall, I noticed how perfectly they were hung on the wall behind his desk. They all had the same brown colour frame and were all of the exact sizes. His coffee was on the table. It was freshly brewed and sweltering. I saw the steam coming from the mug, and the coffee smelt so strong that I could taste it in my mouth.

Finally! There came Dr. Jones, "Hey Ousha," he said with his deep voice as he walked in. He looked stressed and in a rush. He sat down, took a sip of his coffee, then leaned forward with his elbows on the desk and took a deep breath. 'Ousha,' he said, staring at me with a smile that did not seem quite right. It was not the same smile I usually get.

He said, "you have been a very valued member of this business, I have admired all your hard work, and all the work you have done for us is much appreciated," then he took another deep breath.

Have you ever been in a situation where what you thought would happen and the total opposite happened?

Well, that's what happened to me.

He said, "I have some sad news to tell you. The business has not been doing very well. With all the immigration rules, the company is not going to sustain much longer. Therefore, I am going to have to let you go. We have no choice but to make you redundant as effective from now. There was just silence in the room.

I just looked at him quietly, I was in shock, and I could not speak.

Then he carried on, "There is no easy way to say this, but we cannot offer you any redundancy package. We are simply not in the position to do so".

I was in shock and confused. I walked back to my desk feeling lost. I was not sure what to do, but the only thing that was clear to me was that I did not want to go home. So, I decided to stay in the building, desperately searching for jobs online. I was looking for anything, and anywhere I could start as early work as Monday. I did not find anything but the awkward moment came when I realised I was the last person in the building.

I had no choice but to leave.

As I walked to the train station, I was still in shock and confused, but the strongest feeling was the fear of telling my husband Rob that I had lost my job. I decided that perhaps if I called him, it might be easier to give him the bad news rather than tell him face to face.

So that I didn't lose my telephone signal, I stood in front of the train station and did what most good wives would do. I called my husband to tell him what had happened, hoping for support.

He replied:

"What? You lost your job! You are so useless, you are so ugly and black that no one would want to hire you!

What do you have?

You don't even have a job, you don't have a dad, you are an orphan, no one cares for you, no one loves you.

Look at me, I have everything, what do you have? You lost your job and now you can't contribute to the bills, you are useless

Do me a favour, just disappear from this world, don't come home!"

Have you ever felt like your world has fallen apart, leaving you stuck and not knowing what to do?

With a heavy heart, I took a deep breath and carried on walking. I did not know how I got there, but I found myself at the platform where I usually take the train home.

I felt lost. I stood on the platform staring at the yellow line (a demarcation between the train rail and passengers embarking on the train).

All I could hear was Rob's voice, his constant abuse, the train station was so noisy, people rushing around, it was Friday night happy hours after all!

As I carried on staring at the yellow line, a group of girls walked in front of me. I noticed that they all had high heels, dressed up to go out, had beautiful makeup on, and all their hair looked beautiful. They seemed so happy and excited. Some of them had a bottle of coke in their hands, but I could smell something else in there!

Whatever it was, I wished I had some because I was feeling down, helpless, sad, lost, and felt that my life had no worth, I could not feel my legs, and I felt so much emotional pain due to helplessness and despair, and sadness.

Have you ever had a time in your life when you had an important decision to make?

I wished all the pain and noise could go away! Then I thought,

'perhaps if I jumped in front of the train, all the pain would disappear!'

When emotion is high,
intelligence is low. When we feel sad, angry, and frustrated it prompts the brain to go fight or flight mode.

The fight mode will have highly expressive negative thoughts and behaviour. Our thinking brain will be foggy, causing us to have less self-control and less judgment, prompting us to make wrong decisions and actions.

When we are in flight mode, we will have calmer behaviour.

The faster we intervene, the quicker we will regain our intelligent thoughts that will impact our feelings, which will prompt us to take the right actions and achieve positive results.

"No matter what situation you are in, never let your emotions overpower your intelligence."
Kushandwizdom

The SIMBA way

> "Out of the ashes of this tragedy, we shall rise to greet the dawning of a new era."
>
> Scar

In the following chapters, I will share with you my personal story using the SIMBA way. I attended a three days business training course in July 2021 with my mentor Jessen James Chinnapan. He gave me the light bulb moment when he mentioned the journey of Simba in The Lion King, a metaphor with a powerful message, "his purpose is greater than his own self".

When I went home, I was still buzzing from the mind-blowing training I had, and I could not stop thinking about the lessons and the light bulb moments he shared during the course. The same week I watched the movie again and had a completely different perception of the story, and I was inspired by almost thirty-five powerful life and motivational messages.

Simba's inspiring journey from a life of principles, purpose, and selflessness turned into a blind bliss of hedonism, anarchism, narcissism, and purposelessness. This is a true representation of the slippery slope fallacy that victimises people around the world. Nonetheless, Simba was able to regain his kingdom and defeat evil.

It was a wake-up call to become more vigilant towards deceptive behaviour. The metaphor took me straight back to my life a decade ago.

The story is ideal for 'Trauma can be Treatment' with the right guidance, belief, and mindset.

I could relate this to my own life with the most powerful message, which is the emphasis on the circle of life and 'The SIMBA way' was born.

I will share details of my life events in each of the five chapters adopting 'The SIMBA way,' Self, Impact, Mindset, Belief, and Action. Each chapter is embedded with a message, strategy to survive, overcome an abusive relationship, and difficult situations in life that divert individuals from their purpose.

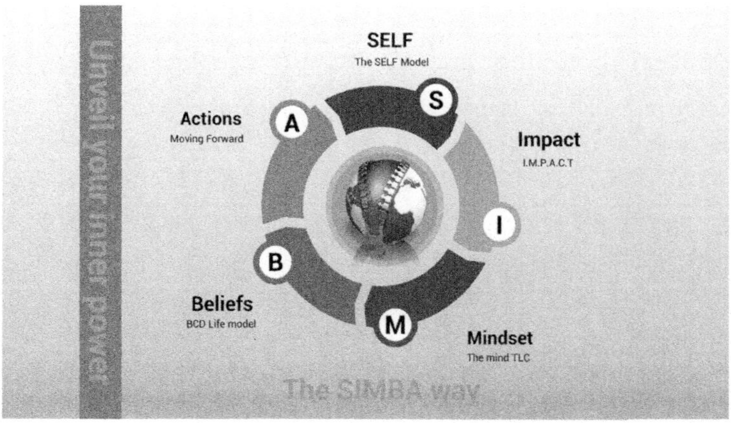

CHAPTER 1

SELF

"Don't change so
people will like you;
be yourself and the
right people will love
you."

Unknown

The Pure love

> "Where there is pure love, there is no room for anger of any kind."
>
> Harold Klemp

My story begins on the beautiful island of Mauritius, where I was born the seventh child, the lucky number seven, making me the youngest out of three brothers and three sisters. My dad passed away, leaving my mum, a beautiful young widow in her mid 30's with seven children, without education and not much support.

My mum, the most powerful woman I know, dedicated all her life to looking after her seven children to the best of her ability. Despite facing many challenges, she never complained, always showered us with love, fed us on time, and always taught us goodness. She always tried to make people happy, and with all the hardship she has been through, she always kept a smile on her face.

I was only four years old when I lost my father, but I was very fortunate that my brothers and sisters stepped up and took the role of parents upon themselves. Their love, attention, and care never made me feel like I had no dad.

Instead, I felt like I had three mums and three dads. I felt loved, lucky, and spoiled rotten. I always felt safe and so well protected that I never even had to deal with any nastiness, or bad people, in fact, I didn't even have to speak for myself. I was wrapped in this bubble of love and protection. I have always been grateful for their pure unconditional love, and I respect them all very much.

I have always been around positive people, and it is in my culture, we respect older people and do not argue or talk back to them. Even when we disagreed, we would never say anything. My love for my brothers was strong. They treated me with so much love that I never disobeyed them. I always listened and trusted all the decisions that were made for me.

I had so much fun growing up. I was full of confidence, extremely happy, and had a cheerful and loving life. I led a carefree life.

When I completed my GCSEs and A levels, I decided to continue Higher Education in the UK. My family supported me, and my big brother Vinay supported me financially to fulfill my dream of pursuing higher education. I arrived in the UK in January 2003. I was also fortunate to have lived with my family Sheela, Mahen, and their daughter Lovena before moving on to live independently. They loved and cared for me as their daughter during my stay there, and they spoiled me rotten.

I worked and studied very hard and was elated when I graduated. I was always fond of studying and continued further studies to achieve postgraduates and master's degrees.

The Poisonous love

"Don't expect true love from fake people."
Unknown.

I had heard of Rob through my family in the UK. We were invited to his wedding on two occasions with two different women, and both weddings were cancelled at short notice. Then one day, through a conversation with my family member, he enquired about me, and after that, I was introduced to Rob. He called me, we chatted, and he said he wanted to meet up.

I was single and free, so I thought, 'why not?'

We met at Nando's in East London as it was convenient and close. He was dressed smartly. I noticed his shiny shoes, baby blue shirt, and black trousers. He gave me the impression of being responsible, showed respect, and sounded very educated and professional. He carried himself with much pride.

We chatted a lot, he told me he had two sisters in their 40's and 50's, and they all lived together in their parent's house in London. I asked whether his sisters were married, he said they could never find the right match because they have high standards.

I took the opportunity to ask him about his two previous attempts to get married. He told me all about the girls and that the girls' families had issues. He mentioned that the first marriage was cancelled because the girl had cheated on him, and the second wedding was cancelled because the girl's parents wanted to come on honeymoon with them. After that, we changed the topic and carried on chatting about our work. When we were leaving, Rob said that he was interested in meeting me again. I was unsure how I felt about him. However, I just went with the flow.

We met a couple of times. I felt like I was not quite getting attached to him, but he was very keen to keep on dating.

In only a couple of months, he said he wanted to marry me. I told him that I did not love him yet, and he surprised me when he said, "that's okay, love can come after the wedding". He did not let go and was quite persistent about it.

He displayed a very caring character, always available when I needed him, sometimes a bit too available where he would even want to join me when I went to meet my girlfriends. He wanted to get involved in everything that I do.

He made various kind gestures like insisting that I should use his spare contracted phone. He always wanted to know where I was and if I had safely reached my home every day. He would be angry if I did not call him or text him late, telling me I should have been home earlier.

I found his actions, anger, jealousy, obsession, always wanting to be around me and involved in everything I do like a sweet, loving, and caring trait.

Time went by, and it's been a year since we started dating. Both sides of our family knew we were dating. In our culture, once the family knows we are dating, it is expected that the relationship is serious.

More is caught than taught. No one taught me this, but from what I saw, observed, and felt when I was growing up, I did not think there was any other way but to take the relationship more seriously. I thought that he must be the one since he was of the same religion as me, was educated and a professional, had a Mauritian background, seemed caring, told me that he loved me and was very keen on getting married.

What else could one want?

He ticked all the boxes. However, I still had a strange feeling, but I did not know what it was.

I tried to explain that feeling to one of my brothers, but we thought perhaps I was overthinking it since I was not clear. Rob kept on insisting that we should get married and as I was turning 30, I knew the family was also expecting me to settle down soon. At this point, it was a feeling of obligation rather than being in love with him.

Regardless, I thought, why not?

So, I asked him to come to meet me, and I said: "Okay, I will marry you!"

He was very excited, and could not wait to inform his parents. A week later, his parents wanted to come to visit where I lived. It was a rainy evening when they arrived at my house. I ran out with an umbrella to escort them into the house so they wouldn't get soaked. They appreciated the gesture. Everything went well that evening.

Soon after, they invited me to their house in London. Rob said that his family wanted to know a bit more about me. When I arrived at his parents' house, they gave me a warm welcome, served me a nice cup of tea and sweets, and then they started asking many questions.

They wanted to know where and what studies I had done, what level, where I had worked, where all my siblings live, what they do, and many other questions. I found it quite exhausting, but I did not mind it as I was keen for them to know me.

Within months, I WAS TOLD that we were getting married in Mauritius. I felt a bit overwhelmed that things were happening so quickly. I had to gather some money as soon as possible to send to Mauritius to support in covering some costs of the marriage. My other siblings also wanted to contribute towards the costs too.

Within very short notice of the time, his parents travelled to Mauritius to make the wedding arrangements. Rob's family met up with my family in Mauritius to discuss the wedding preparations.

I felt like I was on a fast-moving train at top speed, and I could not get off at a stop. Suddenly, I felt I had no control or no say over my wedding.

Things were happening at a fast pace. Since my family is quite big, there have been quite a lot of weddings within the family. There were good communications with some venues that my family already had a connection with. I was informed that there were some disagreements about the venue chosen by my family.

Rob's parents soon started being very rude. They were disrespectful to my family, talked down about the venues suggested, and the people we knew. They said that their son is a prince and needs to be married in a more luxurious venue. We had not yet accumulated all the money to the set budget, but his parents were demanding a contribution for a luxury venue, and they wanted it NOW!

Rob's parents put my family in Mauritius under much pressure and threatened to cancel all arrangements if the money was not given within the same week. I was furious when I heard how they behaved, and I was ready to stop the wedding plan, but Rob promised that he would sort things out.

Despite their rudeness, my family was very tolerant and patient and carried on being respectful as that's how we have always been taught and brought up. Eventually, the money was gathered, their preferred venue was confirmed, which calmed the situation down. A couple of months later, the wedding took place.

We were given our honeymoon package in a beautiful resort in Mauritius as a gift by one of Rob's mum's sisters. On the first day at the hotel, as I walked on the sand with my bikini, I noticed some familiar faces passing close to the restaurant.

"Oh my god", I told Rob, "is that your parents?" He did not look surprised.

His parents and two sisters were also there. I felt a bit embarrassed as I was not dressed appropriately. We received calls from his family during the whole stay telling us when to come for breakfast, lunch, and dinner together at the hotel.

Oh well, once the 'in-laws honeymoon' period was over, we returned to their relative's house. His phone kept on ringing. I saw the same girl's name repeatedly but did not think much of it as there were only a few days left till we had to go back to the UK.

Within a blink of an eye, it was time to go back to the UK! I had not seen where we would stay, as he said that it was a surprise.

When we landed in the UK, we headed to this beautiful house in London which was only five minutes walk from his parents' house. The whole family was there to welcome us. The house was decorated with flowers, balloons, and confetti on the floor, and the bed was already made for us.

There was a handmade pillow. It was very long, which meant that I had to share the same pillow as Rob. That was thoughtful and nice, and I felt fortunate. It all seemed like a dream.

Whenever I asked Rob any questions about the house, he told me, "go ask mum and dad". I did not feel comfortable asking anything. I felt grateful for the gestures and efforts that were done, for having a house to live in, and for the warm welcome.

It was an exciting time when we had to unpack and arrange our belongings. The house had a lot of storage space which made it easy to tidy things up. Rob told me that I should give him all my important documents, including my passport, to give them to his parents to keep safe. I did not feel comfortable doing so; hence he instructed me to keep them in our bedside cabinets to be easily accessible.

I still had some time off, while Rob had to resume work the next day. I thought I could sort out the house and garden.

That week, his mother took me by surprise when she used her own keys and came into the house.

I did not think too much of it as I was just grateful and happy to see her. As she walked in, she looked around the house and gave me some instructions on how the house should be arranged. I kindly took her advice like the good girl I have always been and moved things around to her liking.

Before leaving, she gave me an outfit to wear for an event they were arranging to welcome me into their family. I thought it was thoughtful of her to think of what I should wear.

When we visited family or went out to any functions, I was always surrounded by the in-laws, I was never left alone. Although I thought that was sweet, I felt very uncomfortable as I could not speak openly and freely to other guests.

I felt like I was being watched all the time.

I felt uncomfortable, and I could not be myself. This happened a couple of times, where I was given my outfits for family functions and was always under supervision. His sisters were always concerned that I had everything that I had been given on. It was like they needed me to look good and up to their standards. It was almost like they wanted to show me off and look good in society.

Rob's two older sisters showed a lot of nervousness around their mother.

They were petrified of her and gave me the impression that I should be scared too!

The Money-sucker

> "If you want to know what a man is really like, take notice of how he acts when he loses money."
>
> Unknown

From the first month of our wedding, Rob told me that we needed some cash because we needed to have a family function to welcome me to the family, and he escorted me to the ATM to withdraw the money.

He insisted that he wanted to see my balance.

He wanted to know how much money I had. Rob made me take all the money out at the end of the month when I got paid. He demanded that I should pay him more money in contributing to the housekeeping. I did not mind that, and I was content to contribute.

The problem was the way he was harassing me for it.

All the bills were under Rob's mother's name, and I had no access to anything at all. Furthermore, I never got to see any utility bills or information about the house or what I was paying for.

Rob was verbally aggressive and harassed me, telling me I had to give him the money. He would say "I need it RIGHT NOW".

I was not earning much at that time. He was getting angry despite being fully aware of how much I was earning before the wedding.

When we agreed on how much I could afford to contribute, he told me that I was a fake employee and that all my qualifications were invalid. That's why I was not earning enough.

I felt perplexed, and I was shocked about his behaviour because there were no prior conversations or communications of what is expected of me. Instead, there were constant aggressive demands.

He became very aggressive and had control over my finances, but very secretive over his own.

I soon started feeling very stressed and anxious. I felt that I had lost all the confidence I had and began to believe that there was something wrong with me because I was not meeting his and his family standards.

He said, "you are the dark sheep in the family. Look at us. We all have great jobs with good salaries; you earn peanuts!"

Through a conversation with him later, I tried to tell him that the way he was talking to me was wrong, but he disagreed. He said that the amount of money I was earning was shameful and unacceptable in his surroundings.

He informed me that his family used to call him the dark sheep of the family because he had a lower income than his two sisters. He was pushed to step up, and now he has a better job that pays him better. He said that was the only way to change my job and do better in my life.

I disagreed because I would have accepted to change careers even if he said it more respectfully. I did not think that aggressiveness, rudeness, and control were suitable approaches to help someone step up.

However, this seemed to be his and his family's typical approach. He was not happy that I confronted him and his approach to dealing with things. He became verbally abusive, and hence I started to avoid speaking out to keep away from aggressive arguments and confrontation.

Domestic abuse is mostly perceived as verbal abuse or physical assault, but research shows that it occurs financially just as frequently in an unhealthy relationship.

Financial abuse seldom happens in isolation. Forms of financial abuse may vary from situation to situation.

In some extreme cases, this can lead to threatening violence, and in some cases, this can start subtly, and some people may not be aware of the financial abuse happening to them.

Regardless of the situation, it often involves controlling someone's money, resources, manipulation, demands, and intimidation to keep them weak, controlled, and trapped in the relationship.

Domestic abuse
can happen to women of all income levels,
not just because of their low income.

If you have your own money, you can always get out but not having any financial security makes it almost impossible.

Often when a victim tries to take control of finances back, the situation can escalate and intensify, causing other forms of abuse.

I found that the main reason I was going through financial abuse was to stop me from living an independent life and stay in the relationship under Rob's and his family's control.

How do you know if you are being financially abused:

- Someone has control over your finances. For example, controlling your income, how much you spend, where you spend your money, and what you spend your money on.
- Someone demands your salary the minute you receive it.
- Someone questioning your spending such as where, when, what, and how you spend your money.
- Need to ask permission all the time before using any money
- Start threatening if money issues are challenged or questioned.

Whatever situation you may be in, you can get out of it. We are all bound to meet with bad problems, and the wrong things are bound to meet us. However, when things are not right, you do not need to stay in the wrong. You can make things right, and fortunately, you do not need to do it alone. Some advocates and organisations can provide support. You can also speak to people you trust.

The control freaks

> "People who are the most difficult to please are often the least worth pleasing."
>
> Unknown

It had been almost two months since we got married. As newlyweds, Rob and I were receiving invitations from couples of similar ages to us, but Rob's parents were getting offended that they were also not invited.

Moreover, whenever we wanted to have any guests around, Rob told me to ask his mother first. I felt uncomfortable asking permission about every little thing, and I did not think it was right. Hence, the best option was to avoid inviting people around and decline invitations.

One evening, Rob and I invited his family for dinner. The evening went very well, and I was excited to welcome and serve them food. They all seemed to have enjoyed the food and had a great time. His sisters stayed behind and helped me put the dishes away. We had a good laugh, and they all seemed pleased.

The next day when I visited Rob's parents, I was told that I should learn how to cook to make Rob food the way he likes it. Rob never had a conversation with me about the food I make at home; hence, I was surprised as I had assumed that the evening went well.

> *'It came to my knowledge that he had been complaining to his parents that he did not like the food I made for him. But he never said anything to me. I did not overthink it, as I was keen to learn new recipes.'*

I was excited because I like to learn new things and was happy to do anything to please him and his family. When his mother was teaching me how to cook, she did not like how I was cutting the vegetables, I had to cut some vegetables, and she wanted me to cut them exactly the way she usually does.

I did not mind that '*something new to learn*,' I thought.

That night I learned how to make a particular type of rice that Rob likes to eat. I was thrilled to try it the next day. I got everything right. It smelled amazing. I had all the vegetables and ingredients, and I did exactly what his mother had taught me. That night I went the extra mile by setting the table beautifully.

When he came home, I was excited to serve the food. I was happy and told him, "I hope you are hungry?". He smiled and said, "oh, you cooked", he put his bag on the floor, went around the kitchen, almost like he was inspecting the place.

I served dinner, he looked at his plate, ate one spoon, and then he quietly walked away. It was a while, so I went to look for him. He was not even in the house, I thought, "how quietly did he leave?". A couple of hours later, he came home. I said, "did you go to your parents? Do you want me to warm your food up?"

He said, "No, I have eaten already. I did not like what you made, so I went to mum's to eat".

"What! But I made exactly what your mum usually makes for you, and you love it!" I said.

He responded, "No, it was not the same, it is not even the same colour!"

I did not say anything and just packed all the food away. I took some to work the next day and shared with colleagues who, to my surprise, said how tasty it was.

> *'He just wanted to make a fuss because it was delivered differently to the way his mother usually does. I realised it did not matter what I did, he was never going to be happy or recognise my efforts, and no matter how hard I tried, he already had set his mind to make me unhappy and to be complaining about me all the time.'*

The next day, as there was still some leftover food, I was confused about what to serve, as I could not understand what would make him happy. I feared disappointing him again if I cooked anything he did not like, so I thought I would go for the safe option and have oven food, chicken pie.

When I served the food, he looked furious. He said, "I am going to my mum's". He did not tell me if I should eat or wait, so I assumed that he would probably go to eat there like he always does.

When I sat down to start eating my pie, he put his fingers in my food and laughed. It made me very angry, but I could not react because I was in shock.

When he left, I looked at my food. I did not feel hungry anymore. I cried.

To find true happiness,
we have to be true to ourselves by living our dreams and feeling proud of ourselves rather than being pressured to meet 'certain' standards.

I started to feel that I could not be myself or do things my way because I had to make much effort to fit in and live up to their standards.

Remember that each individual has their version of 'normal,' so none is right or wrong.

We should not expect ourselves to all be alike, but rather respect our differences and value our qualities despite their differences, and those who do not appreciate that should not be in your life!

Be yourself and don't let anyone change you.

The cheater

> "Most people cheat because they focus and pay more attention to what they don't have rather than what they already have."
>
> Unknown.

Rob was angry all the time, I felt that he was hiding things from me, but I could never understand his attitude and behaviour. He was constantly on the phone, leaving the house very early and coming home very late on many occasions.

I have very strong intuition. I had some strange feelings whenever I saw his phone, I could hear my heart beat faster, and I would feel restless. One day, he passed me his phone to talk to his sister, and when I was on the phone, a message popped up from a girl.

It read, "It was fun. When are we meeting up again?"

My hands started shaking, I could hear my heartbeat, and I suddenly felt furious.

I managed to open his messages with shaky hands and was shocked when I saw many messages from other girls.

As I stood in shock, he suddenly came into the room. He snatched his mobile phone off me, quickly scrolled through his phone, and deleted the messages. I asked him what were these text messages about. He said they were old messages from years ago.

I knew he was lying as one of the messages was received when I had the phone in my hand.

I told him that I would inform his parents, and he said, "go ahead, you don't have any proof anyway!"

> *I never thought I'd be the kind of person who would stay with a cheater, but I was committed to the marriage.*
>
> *I wanted it to work!*
>
> *I did not want to give up, and I felt that the relationship was worth saving.*

Like Tony Robbins says, it's in the moment of decision that our destiny is shaped. I decided not to say anything to his parents but tried to make it work.

I could not understand why he would even cheat because he was the one who was so keen on getting married. He was the one who kept on telling me he loved me and was rushing to get married.

Whenever I confronted him about it, he said, "I will make your life hell if you carry on talking about this".

Finding out that he was cheating, feeling controlled, and constantly stressing about disappointing him and his family for not meeting their standards was changing the person I was.

I was not happy. I was constantly feeling sad, I could not smile, and I did not enjoy life. I did not want to give up on him and still had hope that things would change.

But the situation I was in and his behaviour made me lose my self-belief, thinking that perhaps I was not doing enough and slowly started losing my self-confidence.

I felt that I was responsible for making the situation better. Hence, I started to live life under his and his family's terms and disregarded my own beliefs, needs, and wants.

The more I tried to make it work, the lonelier and sadder I felt.

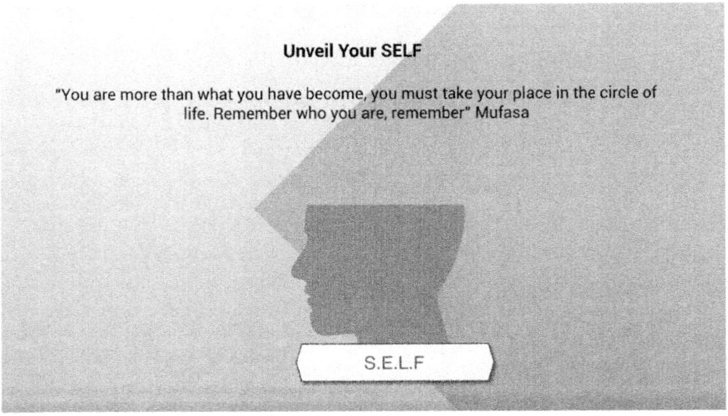
Unveil Your SELF
"You are more than what you have become, you must take your place in the circle of life. Remember who you are, remember" Mufasa
S.E.L.F

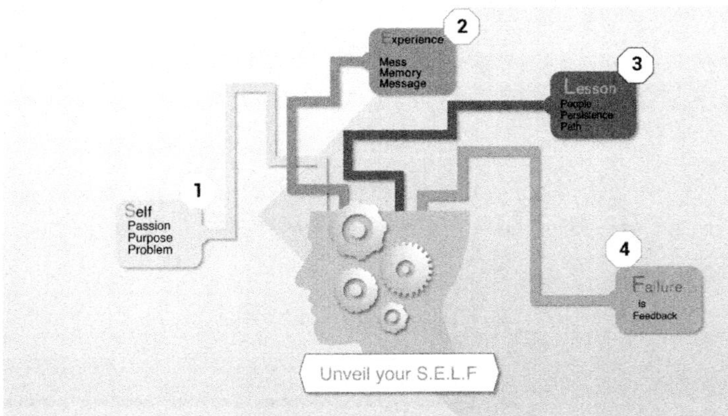
1
Self
Passion
Purpose
Problem
2
Experience
Mess
Memory
Message
3
Lesson
People
Persistence
Path
4
Failure
is
Feedback
Unveil your S.E.L.F

1. SELF

Problematic situations and toxic people can make you feel like there is something wrong with you. There is nothing wrong with you!

Life is not about sacrificing yourself to please others. It would be best if you were changing yourself for the better, not for the worse.

If you feel circumstances and people around you are changing who you are, then start asking yourself these questions:

Who am I?

What makes my life worth living?

How would you like to be remembered?

What is my purpose in life?

What makes me happy?

What are the problems that I had and have already solved?

How did I solve these problems?

How do I feel right now?

Who are the people that are making me feel that way?

2. Experience

Our previous experiences are what shaped our lives and the person we are until this point. Both the positive and negative experiences become ingrained in us and are fundamental to our happiness and wellbeing.

Like it or not, we have to work backwards and understand our previous experiences to move forward. Asking the following questions will allow you to tap into your past experiences, which can help you know how you feel or behave in your current situation.

What are the good experiences in my life?

How did they make me feel?

What experiences/problems did I have that are similar to the one I have now?

How did I overcome them?

What is this that you did not forget?

If you were someone else, what advice would you give yourself?

3. Lessons

There are no regrets in life apart from all the lessons learned. Our life is our best teacher, and sometimes things or situations in life will keep on repeating until the lesson is learned.

If you are unable to resolve your current issues, then ask yourself the following questions:

What lesson did you learn from your previous problems?

Who are the people who got you into a mess?

Who are the people who got you out of a mess?

How did patience reward you?

What problems do you have right now?

Who do you have around you that can support you?

Who are the people that bring the worst out in you?

Who are the people who bring the best out of you?

Whom can you trust?

What path are you taking right now?

What would you do differently?

4. Failure

One of the hardest things to do in life is to start all over again. Everybody fails but doesn't like to admit it. There is no failure; instead, there is feedback. There are three types of failures.

The first one is preventive, where you could have prevented failure but did not do anything about it. The second one is unavoidable when things are not in your control, and the third one is intelligent failures that arise through deliberate, thoughtful actions.

Regardless of the categories of failures, each of them gives you feedback on what you did right and what you did wrong.

Ask yourself the following questions:

What made me fail?

How did I feel when I failed?

What can I do to make it better?

What did I learn from this failure?

CHAPTER 2

IMPACT

"Nobody likes conflict, but sweeping issues under the rug ultimately causes more damage than addressing things directly."

Unknown

Being in an abusive relationship can devastate someone's life now and in the future. Many people do not realise how damaging this can be, how it can influence the quality of their lives, their wellbeing, and the consequences on people around them or their mental health.

Below I share the impact that being in a toxic and abusive relationship had on me:

Isolation
Mental stress
Physical pain
Anxiety
Control
Trauma

ISOLATION

> "A healthy relationship will never require you to sacrifice your friends and family."
>
> Ousha Demello

Whenever any member of my family called, Rob would refuse to talk to them and always told me to hurry up and be furious with an attitude like I was disturbing him. He showed no respect or interest in how my family was but instead, complained to his parents that I was on the phone to my mum, brothers, or sisters.

His mum told me that I should not be calling my family, that she does not call hers, as her marital family is now her prominent family.

She said, "why do you have to talk to your family? They are not your family anymore. We are your priority, they don't care about you anymore, no one cares for you, you only have us now".

I knew they were wrong, but they made me feel like I was committing a crime when communicating with my family and relatives. I eventually reduced contact, but now and then, I would hide and call my mum and siblings, because I was too scared the situation would become abusive again. I tried to do everything the way they liked to please them.

I did not know how to tell my family what was happening. I was worried that things might get worse if I said anything, so I avoided their calls. I would always lie and say that I was busy. Sometimes when I received a phone call, especially if Rob knew it was one of my girlfriends, he would answer the phone to say that I was busy and that they should not call me.

Eventually, I slowly started to lose contact with my friends too. Whenever it was safe to, I would call one of my friend Kavish. I started opening up to him about how I was feeling at home.

It had been a while since my family had not heard from me.

One day, I received a text from my brother Vimal who lives in France. As I tried to read his message, Rob aggressively asked me who it was. I told him it was my brother, and while I was replying to his message, Rob wanted to know what I had typed. He desperately wanted to read my message, so he tried to get my phone off me.

He was being aggressive, so I told him to leave me alone. "I'm just texting my brother", I told him. He did not believe me, and he wanted to see for himself.

I refused to give him my phone as I said I was texting my brother, and I've got the right to do so. He started calling me names, he called me a liar, and I said I wasn't texting my brother.

I felt suffocated because he was keeping tabs on me like I was some toddler. The trust in the relationship was not the healthiest, and the reasons were absurd. He was always worried that I would cheat on him because his previous fiance had, and he most probably because he was cheating himself.

He was imparting all the bad experiences with his last broken relationships with other women, not realising that he had married someone genuine and had a good wife who was ready to do anything to make things work. I am not an argumentative person, but I was in constant fear of any small situation turning into an abusive situation.

As I refused to give him my phone, he pushed me and snatched my phone from my hand. He read my brother's message to me, and then he threw my phone back at me. He made it clear that I should not be communicating with my family.

The following day, when I grabbed my phone, I found that there was something wrong. I could not understand as it was on charge during the night. I realised that he had deliberately taken the battery off the phone. When I asked him why he did it, he said, well, you broke it yourself.

I felt helpless living there. On other occasions when I would use my laptop, he would take my charger away and sometimes hide it.

I did not know why he was doing it.

All I know is that he was determined to make my life a living hell because I confronted him about cheating.

> "Me, myself and I, sometimes I laugh, sometimes I cry, yet I should never ever deny, me, myself and I…"
>
> Jackie Latty

Isolation is a sign of abuse.

Passive-aggressive behaviour is a sign most commonly attempted to isolate a person to exert control.

Being isolated can make you feel lonely and vulnerable. Not being able to talk to your loved ones, having people to check on your safety and wellbeing can cause anxiety and stress.

These signs are more likely to go unnoticed, further increasing vulnerability to repeat abuse and harm.

An abuser will control whom you see, whom you talk to, monitor your ongoing and outgoing calls, cut you off from your friends and family or even damage your relationship with others.

Isolation is not loneliness. If you feel isolated, remember that you are not lonely. Instead, you are spending time alone. Take the opportunity to connect with Yourself and start taking control of your feelings so that you can change the script.

Jessica Nutter

Mental Stress

> "All stress, anxiety, depression, is caused when we ignore who we are, and start living to please others."
>
> **Paulo Coelho**

As the months went by, the fear, the anxiety, and the stress became worse with his constant abuse. Rob would swear at me if I were five minutes late, saying I was cheating on him.

I felt so helpless that I did not know what to do or how stop all the mental torture. Things seemed to escalate in the worst way possible. His behaviour was getting more and more aggressive. He would get angry over anything small.

One of the months I got paid £100 less and therefore had to pay him £100 less. He told me that I should f*** off from the house because I am unreliable.

That month he didn't let me use the washing machine. He told me that I was a squatter in his home because I could not pay the right amount. I had no right to put the heating on.

He was constantly abusive in his language, tone and behaviour, always talking me down. He repeatedly told me that there was something very wrong with me, that's why I was not being paid enough. He said nobody wanted to employ me and pay me a decent salary because my qualifications were invalid. He complained that I was fake for the reason that I was hideous and dark.

One of Rob's relatives was going to travel abroad to Mauritius. I knew she would meet my mum. You see, my mum's birthday was approaching soon in a month, so I thought I would send her a birthday card and a gift of £50. That meant that I would be £50 short of paying him that month.

He went to complain to his mother and father that I had sent money for my mum.

They came to the house and started humiliating me, his mother said "When was the last time you gave us any money as a gift? You don't do anything and contribute to anything here, and why are you sending money abroad to your family. We are your family, not them anymore!"

They carried on humiliating me and made me feel guilty for sending £50 to my mum.

I could not respond as I was shocked and confused as I would give Rob all my money at the end of the month. So, he probably did not tell them that I do contribute. I could not even utter a word as I was feeling in a defeated state of mind.

Mental torture
is far more painful than physical abuse, we can heal a broken bone in a month, but it's much harder to heal a broken mind.

A person does not need to raise their hand or even voice to be an abuser. The abuse can manifest in how they treat and talk to you and their expectations of you.

Abusers will use tactics to undermine your self-esteem, such as name-calling, telling, patronising, embarrassment, sarcasm, insults, pushing your buttons, blame, manipulation, threats, financial control, and unpredictable behaviours.

All these can chip away your self-esteem and make you doubt your perception and reality. Your mental health is key to your everyday life. Mental stress will affect how we feel, how we behave, and how we cope in life.

A good
and mentally healthy person will never torture others.

It is usually the tortured that becomes the torturer if they are given the platform to do so.

No matter who this person may be, you do not deserve it.

IT IS NOT YOUR FAULT.

Physical Pain

> "Returning an insult for insult is justice, returning injury for insult is injustice."
>
> Unknown.

As days, weeks and months went by, he was getting more and more abusive. It was becoming a regular thing for him to have mean and aggressive behaviour. I lived in constant fear of doing or saying anything because he would get angry over anything small.

It was like this ticking bomb that was ready to explode at any moment.

One day, as my phone rang, I saw that it was my brother from France. I did not answer as I was very uncomfortable talking in front of Rob. I cut the phone off, but he rang again.

Rob ran towards me and said, "Who is it? What are you hiding? you cheating b****, what have you been up to?"

I told him it was my brother and that I preferred to talk to him the next day as it was getting late. He demanded that I give him my phone to check who it was. I refused to hand it to him because I felt safe having my phone with me, knowing that I could communicate with my family.

He wrestled me down, trying desperately to get my phone.

As I resisted, he sprained my waist with so much strength that I had to let go of the phone. I started crying as my hand was in a lot of pain.

I told him that my hand was hurting a lot. He realised what he had done and quickly went to get ice. He said, don't worry, the pain will go away, you won't even need a doctor.

> *'I thought he cared, but all he was worried about was that I would need to see a doctor. Hence, he was trying to help me for his own good.'*

The next day, my hand was still hurting badly. I told him that I would need to go to the doctor. He told me I should tell the doctor that I had sprained my hand trying to lift a table. I nodded, got ready, and went.

On my way, I found it hard to decide whether I should tell the truth or lie.

I stood outside the surgery, thinking very deeply. Then I decided I should tell the truth, and then Rob might understand that he should not hurt me again.

When I went for the consultation, I told the doctor how it happened and opened up how I was being treated at home. I told the doctor that I didn't want this to be recorded as I wanted things to work out. If Rob knew that I spoke the truth, it would make things even worse for me. Hence, I did not want him to take anything further.

He then advised me that I should have a bag ready, with all my important documents like passport, bank cards, and some money hidden somewhere in case I need to leave urgently one day.

When I came home, the first thing Rob asked was, "Did you tell the doctor about the table?"

I took a deep breath, and I could not lie.

I said, "No, I told him the truth!". He did not say a word.

He just left the house and disappeared for hours again. He was at his parent's house again. The next day, his parents and his sisters came to the house. They all looked outraged.

The mother said to me, "Are you disabled? Why do you go to the doctor's so often? Look at me, at my age. I never visit doctors. It is very shameful that you go to the doctors all the time. You should be ashamed of yourself. You are young and yet such an unhealthy person".

They all looked so angry like they wanted to kill me. I sat down quietly while they were all humiliating me. It would not matter what I said. I would be wrong anyway, so staying quiet was the best option.

That same week, he came home a bit late, saying that he had gone to visit the doctors due to feeling too stressed.

'He had already been planning his combat in case the matter of him hurting me escalated.'

On another occasion, when he was using the bathroom, one of my siblings texted me to make sure I was okay. I quickly read the message, and I was replying when he came back to the bedroom.

He asked who it was, and when I told him it was my family, he said, "why are you contacting your family? I will tell my parents and shame you".

He asked to see my phone, and when I said no, he pushed me on the bed, pinned me down with his knees on my chest, held my hand very tight, and snatched my phone away. I begged him to give it back. He just laughed.

I felt safer when I had my phone with me. That was the only way I felt I could reach out to my siblings. Even if they were far away, I felt safe when I spoke to them.

When I went to work, I went to a phone shop and got a new cheap phone and sim card. I thought, just in case I don't get my phone back, at least I would have a spare one to call my family secretly.

When I came home, I placed the phone in a plastic bag and left it underneath the bin outside the house. I walked into the house frightened again that evening. He told me that he would give me my phone back, but with the condition that I should not be communicating with my family. I agreed.

I could not even ask his family to help me as they also did not want me to communicate with my immediate family or friends.

Denial is a coping
mechanism that a person uses to adjust to
a particular situation.

Refusing to acknowledge that something is
wrong and accepting the truth is a bad way
of coping with any situation.

I denied the fact that I was in an abusive
relationship, thinking that things could
change.

That denial was impacting my mental
health. It became a barrier to seeing what
was right and wrong, still believing that it
was not his fault.
It's mine.

You can determine
whether your partner is violent simply by
asking yourself the following questions:

- Has he ever trapped you in a room and not let you out?
- Has he ever threatened to hurt you?
- Has he ever shoved, grabbled, or poked you?
- Has he ever thrown an object that hurt or could have hurt you?
- Has he ever raised his fist as if he was going to hit you?

If any of these questions are yes, then s/he has already been violent.

Anxiety

"The quality of your life ultimately depends on the quality of your relationships."

Unknown

On a Saturday morning, I saw that the sun was out during one of the weekends, so I went out and stood where the sun was shining brighter, enjoying the sun on my skin. The sun makes me feel happy. Then I thought I could put the washing out, which I did. Then I spent the day cleaning the house.

Rob would usually go to his parent's house for the whole day every Saturday while I stayed in the house to do the routine cleaning.

On that day, Rob returned to the house earlier, at three o'clock and said that we should go shopping. I was excited to be able to go out together. While we were out, it started raining. I looked up, felt the rain on my hands, then suddenly I remembered that I had left the washing out.

Rob got annoyed when I told him we should go home because of the washing. Since his mood changed, I was anxious about how he would behave when we got home. I was in constant fear and anxiety.

We returned to the house as quickly as possible as it started to rain heavily. As soon as we entered the house, we placed the shopping on the kitchen work surface. As

I ran outside to get the washing from the washing line, Rob locked me out of the house.

He said, "This is all your fault; why did you put the washing out?"

I suffered from back pain at the time, and I could not handle the cold. I told him to open the door, and he just ignored me. I did not know what to do. I saw my neighbour from their back garden, so I started calling their names, but they could not hear me.

Rob heard me shouting, so he quickly ran to the door and opened it, saying, "what are you doing? Why are you making a scene?".

He asked me if the neighbours had heard me.

I lied and said yes.

His behaviour became strange, like a little boy who had been grounded, walked to his bed, and went to sleep.

> *"Rob was worried that the neighbours had heard me and would know what has been going on in the house."*

That was not the end of it; the next day, his two sisters came into the house to instruct me how to do things around the house, teaching me when to put the washing out, the order of doing house chores, and treating me as if I knew nothing.

> *"He would involve his parents and sisters in every little thing, which made things even more stressful for me to handle.*
>
> *His two sisters were not married. Instead, they kept on interfering in my marital life, making things worse."*

I felt powerless due to constant fear and lamentation. I knew anything could trigger anger, shouting, and abusive language; hence I was constantly worried and nervous about everything.

Being angry seemed to become routine in the house.

Emotional abuse results in anxiety, which causes stress, overthinking and leads to poor self-esteem and confidence, constantly worrying about being hurt.

Constantly worrying about your relationship and your partner's reaction can impact negatively on your quality of life, affect your wellbeing, and in some cases, can cause a nervous breakdown.

Anxiety builds tension leading to negative energy. Hence it is vital to give yourself positive reminders. Some exercises like affirmation and mirror exercises have been included in Chapter 5.

Control

> "When a person attempts to control someone else's life, it only reflects the lack of control they have on their own."
>
> Daniel Chidiac

On a given day, we went to a family function. On the way back, we all travelled together in the car. Rob was driving, his father was in the passenger's seat, his mother, two sisters, and I sat in the back seat. Since I was the slimmest one, I was sitting a little bit more forward.

As I looked out of the window, knowing that he had been cheating and how he was treating me made me feel sorrowful. My eyes filled with tears, and I could not stop them from rolling down my face.

One of his sisters saw me crying and asked me what had happened. I just nodded and said I was okay. When we reached his parents' house, his sisters started running around making us all tea. I helped out, and everything had to be done so perfectly, and quite stressful considering making a cup of tea should be relaxing.

As we sat down at the table, I could not control my emotions. I broke down in tears.

I opened up and told Rob's family that he was cheating and told them about the messages I saw on his phone. They did not say anything. They all stayed quiet.

Rob defended himself, saying that I had been aggressive with him and blamed it all on me, that I was just looking for arguments. He became pretty loud and started saying how much of a bad wife I am, that I don't do anything well and that I am making up stories. He was very dominant, speaking loudly, angrily, with authority, and he behaved like he had all the power and control when he was around his family.

It got late at his parent's house, so Rob and I made our way home. That night I did not sleep at all.

The following day, I had just managed to fall asleep when I heard his mum's voice screaming out loud, "relationship is not all about sex. In this house, things are going to happen MY WAY OR THE HIGH WAY". His mother had let herself into the house when we were still in bed.

I jumped out of bed, confused. I did not understand why Rob's mother had come into the house and started screaming.

'Is she talking to Rob or me?'

It felt like I was the one who was in trouble.

I soon realised that Rob had spent some time with his parents earlier in the morning at their house. I am not sure what he told them, but he did not say anything good about me.

I ran downstairs feeling embarrassed as I had not even brushed my teeth.

She shouted, "it does not matter what my son does outside of this house. As long as he comes back to you, you should be happy. Do you know how lucky you are to have been married to this family? Why can't you appreciate everything we do for you and live happily".

I told her that he comes home late and it is not right what he does.

She replied: "well, don't worry about that, I know who he is with".

It felt like I had no right to know anything, I had no right to express myself, I am just supposed to be quiet and grateful for being married and living in this house.

I felt helpless.

It seemed like he could do what he liked, he could be wrong, and his family will always support and defend him. I had no control over anything, not even my life. They made me feel like I was the wrong one and that I was not good enough.

Your life is too valuable to go through life, allowing people to control you, and you feel guilty. People who try to control you do so out of anxiety that things may go wrong or not their way.

They adopt controlling behaviour to assert dominance and gain power. Control is a form of abuse.

If you find yourself in a situation where you have no control and someone else is showing signs of dominance, you should communicate with other people, seek help and surround yourself with people you trust.

Trauma

> "A house where you do not feel happy, comfortable and safe is not a home."
>
> Ousha Demello

One evening after finishing work, my heart started beating rapidly and loud as I made my way to the house. As I used the key to open the door, my hands were shaking. I was terrified to go in because I never knew what to expect when I got in.

As I entered the house, I noticed that Rob was already home. I heard some noises upstairs, so I went to greet him. He was standing in the bathroom, holding a sponge and looking enraged.

I said, "Hello, are you OK? what are you doing?"

He started shouting very aggressively, "I need you to scrub the bathroom. Can't you see it needs cleaning? You're so useless you did not clean this morning, my mum came to the house during the day, she told me that the house is dirty. You didn't clean the house".

I told him that I had tidied up as much as possible before going to work, and the house was NOT dirty. The only thing was some bread crumbs near the sink because I rushed in the morning. That was it.

I did not realise that his mother came into the house during the day to inspect the house while we are not in and complained to Rob.

> *'I realised that he was furious because of what his mum said to him. I am not sure what conversation they had, but whatever his mum said certainly did not do any good to him, me, or my relationship. I could not understand why his family would not stop interfering, and things only got aggravated whenever they got involved.'*

He started shouting at me, saying that I was useless, why did his mum have to see the house this way and complain to him. He said I was supposed to clean the whole house before leaving to go to work.

He said, "you're the woman; that's what you're supposed to do".

That night his parents came to the house and his mother was complaining about the house, "why were there breadcrumbs in the sink?"

When I said I did not want to be late for work, his dad said, "a woman is supposed to work 27 hours out of 24 hours; you should be on top of everything."

I disagreed with him, but I didn't say a word; I was choked up because of extreme anxiety, and I could not speak back to defend myself.

The pressure was too much, and the atmosphere was too stressful. I was too scared to get any more verbal abuse, so I just agreed to everything they said.

Fear was constant, and I felt like I was living in a world of daily terror. I said I was sorry and I will make sure that the house is clean next time. Every morning I had to wake up and clean the whole house before going to work, and he was also expecting that I would cook dinner by the time he came home.

I did not feel like I had a life, as everything was just about pleasing Rob's family even when they were unfair. They were so unjust and behaved in such a wrong way.

I felt my life was worth nothing.

I started asking myself all sorts of questions. What could I do to make things better? Nothing that I did was good enough or up to 'their standards'.

I was trying so hard and was doing everything they were asking me to do. I was confused because my efforts seemed to go in vain, and I never knew what to do to make them happy.

Approximately 50%
of all individuals will be exposed to at least one traumatic situation in their life. It does not necessarily mean an abusive relationship. It could be harassment at work, bullying, sexual assault, giving birth, being attacked or kidnapped, accidents, and so many more situations where someone feels bullied.

Research has shown that 8% of them will develop posttraumatic stress disorder. Women have more significant risks of negative consequences following trauma. However, some people wait years to receive support, while some move on without any problems.

Living with an abusive person and experiencing emotional abuse can be a traumatic experience and make you feel stressed, lonely, isolated, depressed and anxious about everything.
A toxic relationship can induce hopelessness, powerlessness and fear.

The good news
is that healing is possible with trauma through professional treatment, therapy or medication.

Treatment will vary among different individuals and depend on the severity of the situation.

There are other methods of healing, such as exercise, communication and connection with people, self-care, mindfulness, asking for support and a balanced lifestyle. You do not have to deal with any situation on your own.

More coping strategies are covered in Chapter 5.

CHAPTER 3

MINDSET

"Making the right decision is hard, but usually turns out right. Making the wrong decision is easy, but usually turns out wrong."

Unknown

Gaslighting

> Gaslighting is a form of psychological abuse where a person or a group of people make someone question their sanity."
>
> Marney A. White

Every Saturday, I would make my way to the market to buy fresh vegetables and eggs. I had to pass by the police station and would usually be alone. I used to love going to the market because I used to have a peaceful walk, fresh air and I used to feel a little bit free, even if it was for just one hour.

I often took the opportunity to secretly call my good friend Kavish as that was the only chance I could talk without fear of reprisal.

Talking to him always made me feel better, knowing that he is a phone call away no matter when I need him. I told him everything that was happening. He was such a good friend. He was always there to listen to me. He was frustrated about how Rob was treating me. He advised me that I should report Rob to the police.

I did not think I could ever do that. I never thought that I was going through domestic violence, and I did not believe this could be an option.

"What if they arrest him and he stays in prison?" I said.

I thought I should talk to his family instead and try to get them to help me. That night, I went to Rob's parents' house. I told them that Rob is very aggressive and that he has been very abusive to me and swears a lot in the house. I asked them to help me speak to him and to help him stop behaving the way he does towards me.

His older sister looked at me and said, "why should we help you? You must have done something to provoke him for him to swear at you!"

His parents looked at me with anger, and they were fuming because I had dared to complain about their son. I realised that they were not ready to help me. I said to them that the situation was awful and I did not want to complain to the police.

Rob's father said, "going to the police is not an option. If you go to the police station, you will have to end this relationship. If you ever report my son, we will make sure that you two are divorced".

I did not say anything. I did not know what to say!

While I made my way out of the house, my head was spinning, but I kept walking. I just wanted to get out of there.

As I left the house, I was even more confused. I did not get married to be divorced. I wanted this marriage to work. I became perplexed with fear of being divorced; my heart began to palpitate, I cried in anxiety as if drowning in an ocean of grief.

I realised that no matter how wrong Rob is; they are the ones encouraging it. They are all as bad as each other.

The next time I went to the market, I spoke to Kavish again and told him what happened when I asked his parents to help me. He continuously encouraged me to go to the police station.

I thought, okay, if I get the local authority involved, maybe he will understand that what he is doing is wrong. I don't want him punished. I want him to realise that how he behaves and treats me is wrong, and I want him to stop.

I stood in front of the police station, and I stared at the door for a while. I was still unsure. Then I took a deep breath and with a heavy heart I walked in. As I stood in the reception, I was behind a man who was giving a statement. There were some empty chairs, but I felt uncomfortable sitting there, so I ran out.

I was too worried that I was going to make a big mistake. I stood outside the door, trying to think; my mind was too strained to think.

Then I went back in again; I could not go through with it and walked out again. As I stood by the door, I did not know what the right thing to do was. When I made my third attempt to go in, the police officer did not let me leave; she said she had seen me going in and out and wanted to know how she could help.

I sat down, and I told her that I wanted to make sure that Rob did not get in trouble before I started talking. I explained that it would make me feel better if they knew my situation because I did not feel safe.

I asked her again, saying, "please, I do not mean any harm to Rob or his family. The only reason I am here is for my safety and not to punish him".

She started by asking me for my personal information. Then I ended up telling her everything, from the verbal abuse to the family effort to dissuade me from coming to the police. Before leaving, I told her that I meant no harm and did not want any actions taken.

She told me she could not guarantee anything but assured me that I had done the right thing to come forward.

I went home that day; as usual, not knowing what to expect. I decided to tell him that I had been to the police. But that night, we had to attend a family function, so I could not talk to him because we were rushing to get ready. I was unsure how to tell him, so I thought I would talk to him first thing in the morning. But that morning, he woke up early and rushed out.

In the evening, when I came home from work, I found Rob in bed shivering.

I asked what was going on; he said, "it's you who made me ill, you stress me and now look what happened. I am disappointed in you, you reported me to the police, now I am ill because of you, it's all your fault".

I explained that he was not treating me right, and I had already kindly asked him not to treat me the way he does. Then I went to his parents for support, but no one wanted to know. I tried to clarify that they did not leave me any choice but to get external help.

The next day, Rob's parents asked me to come to their house. His mother, father and two sisters surrounded me, yelling at me, saying that I had backstabbed them, and asking me why I had to go to the police station.

They had a chair in the middle of the living room, and they asked me to sit right in the seat. I felt so intimidated as they started to shout at me, telling me that I was a hypocrite.

I tried to explain that I did come forward to ask for help, but they left me with no choice. I explained I did not mean any harm, but Rob was constantly abusive to me, and they had refused to help me. All I want is for him to stop treating me the way he does.

His parents gave me dirty looks like I had committed a crime as if it was all my fault. They told me that Rob mistreated me because I must have provoked him.

They made me feel guilty, as if I had done something so awful to upset him. They also made me feel like I deserved the way he behaved towards me, the things he said, the names he called me. They did not want to acknowledge that he was abusive and kept on taking his side.

Rob's sister said with a threatening tone, "you hurt my brother; you hurt all of us. This is not over for you".

His mother started calling me many names and said, "I will make you wash my feet and drink that water because that's where you belong, under my feet."

They made me feel that I deserved the humiliation and the shame.

Abusive and toxic
people use gaslighting to gain control by
shaming the person, lying and denying things
that happened.

Typically, poisonous people (could be anyone, partner, partner, family, friend to a coworker) are very good at this and can influence the soundest-minded person to doubt and question their motives and behaviour.

They can make you feel and believe that everything that does not go well is all your fault. They will make you feel confused and make you feel like you are crazy.

They can turn tables around very quickly and know how to pull others off-centre and get into your head.

They will even make you apologise even when you are not wrong.

This can have a significant impact on someone's mental health.

Therefore, if you feel like you are experiencing gaslighting, have a relationship that makes you emotionally exhausted, you need to take care of your mental health before it gets too late. It is okay not to feel okay.

It is all right to feel sad and cry but never blame yourself for how things turned out when the situation was out of your hands.

Know that you are not crazy, don't blame yourself for others inability to care for you. Things can happen which is not your fault. It is not your responsibility to change people or teach them not to be toxic. If you feel things are your fault, then you are being manipulated.

THIS IS TOXIC AND NOT ACCEPTABLE.

It is fundamental to
keep journals, keep voice notes, pictures, or any form of evidence to understand the negative patterns of behaviour.

It will help you know if you are being emotionally abused.

You should keep any evidence in a very safe place, and perhaps you may want to talk about the behaviours and how you feel.

Talk to someone you trust, friends & family, your general practitioner, domestic abuse organisations, or mental health professionals.

The manipulative punisher

> "Any change, even a change for better, is always accomplished by discomforts."
>
> Arnold Bennett

Reporting Rob to the police did not make me feel safer. Instead, it made me feel more vulnerable since the whole family became even more abusive.

Each time I went to his parent's house, they gave me nasty looks and maltreated me. They would say things like, "are you still here? Haven't you left yet?"

I didn't feel safe anymore. I reported Rob to the police hoping that this would help him and that the family understood that what they were doing was wrong.

Instead, I was constantly walking on eggshells. I was even more afraid than before reporting Rob. I did not feel safe at all. The atmosphere was so vile and felt even more poisonous than before. They told me there was only one thing I could do to make things better, that I should go back and withdraw my statement from the police station.

They made me feel guilty, and I had a strong feeling that things would only get worse. I did not know what to do. So, I went back to the police station, and I withdrew the statement. I thought this would make things better, but they started treating me even worse, calling me names and pressurising me to make payments for living in the house in cash every month.

The sisters said I'm worth nothing, "you are an orphan, and no one loves you. Without us, you are a lonely and sad person".

The mother said, "if I had to go back to my family, they would treat you like a dog".

They kept on telling me that I was lucky to have been in their family, as they have high standards, both his sisters and Rob have good jobs, people know them, that they are well off with a good reputation, and if I went back to my family, I would never be happy.

Their behaviours were very contradicting, and they were constantly pushing my boundaries. Rob would find any excuse to start an argument, complain and be angry about the slightest things.

On one occasion when he was angry, again, he said to me, "if you die, no one will ever know because no one loves you, no one cares for you, no one will even ask".

Although they were only words, his words, I was scared. I felt that my life was in danger. I felt miserable and insecure.

I felt that he wanted to punish and hurt me, but he was cautious about it if I reported him again. He was determined to make my life a living hell.

When we slept at night, he took up all the space in the bed and made me feel extremely uncomfortable. I would be hanging on the corner of the bed. I could not sleep well. He made sure to punish me for going to the police station. He ill-treated me to make sure that I knew that I had done wrong. He continuously tried to provoke me to be angry by saying nasty things about me, but I stayed quiet.

He started saying nasty things about my brothers and sisters, criticising them individually and calling them names.

Then he would go on about my sweet mum, saying, "I f****d your mum for ten rupees".

He knew this would hurt me. He would carry on yelling in my ears and wait for me to react. He made sure that I was sad and felt down. He succeeded, as I felt lost most of the time, with no self-esteem and self-worth. I felt paralysed and felt like my life had no purpose.

He would randomly start arguments with me, almost provoking me to react a certain way and say things. He wanted to make me angry, but I felt so emotionally drained that I didn't even have the energy to get angry.

He never seemed to give up, and he carried on being rude. He was manipulative and was hurting my feelings and emotions.

Tic for a Tac

> "An eye for an eye will only make the whole world blind."
>
> Mahatma Gandhi

On a beautiful Sunday, I woke up, pulled the curtains and opened the window. As Rob was in the bathroom, I leaned on the window sill, and I lifted my face to feel the sunshine. I closed my eyes, and I felt peaceful, and the sensation of the sun on my skin made me feel good.

This feeling soon disappeared when I reflected on my current situation.

I did not think I should give up. I thought to myself, 'I can make this better. Perhaps I should try harder. I decided to speak with Rob and tell him that I was sorry for reporting him to the police and ask him if we could perhaps have a fresh start.

When he came out of the shower, Rob started rushing to get dressed to go out. I asked him if we could talk. He ignored me at first and carried on getting dressed while admiring himself in the mirror.

I asked him again; he looked at me and said, "okay". But when we went downstairs, I saw that he was making his way to the door. I asked him what time he was going to be back, but he did not respond. He just ignored me.

I could feel his negative energy and did not feel comfortable touching him; hence I held the tip of his T-shirt, trying to get his attention.

But he just rushed out and slammed the door. I did not understand the problem, but as he is angry most of the time, I thought there would probably be another episode when he returns.

After around an hour later, I heard the door knock. I was not expecting anyone.

I went to the window and peeked outside to see who it was. I could not see very well at first until the person knocking moved back. I was surprised to see two police officers, one male and one female. I thought to myself, 'I have already withdrawn my statement, and I have not returned to report Rob, so why are they here?'

I ran to the door, and little did I know I had yet to have the biggest shock of my life!

I opened the door, smiled at them and asked how I could help them? The female officer asked me if I was Ousha. I said 'yes' in a hesitant way.

They said, "we have just received an allegation against you by your husband, he reported that you had aggressive behaviour and have hurt his arms"

"What?" I said.

Although it was an unpleasant surprise, I could not help but laugh and ask them to come inside. I asked the officers to take a seat and told them that I couldn't believe they were here for something that had never happened.

I told them exactly what had happened and demonstrated how I had 'touched' his T-shirt. It did not take too much convincing; they believed me.

Both Rob and his father came back to the house while the police were still talking to me. His father did not leave my sight, as he was listening to everything I was saying to the police.

I started telling them what had been happening and that I was not the aggressive one and that Rob was the abusive one. His father was standing a short distance behind the policewoman and was frowning at me.

The policeman then took Rob out and warned him for playing Tic for a Tac, and he should not waste police time.

I did not feel safe anymore. I felt that it was all about revenge, and even after I had withdrawn the statement, Rob and his family would want to make me pay for reporting him to the police.

I took the courage to admit that I could not handle this situation on my own. So, I called my brother Vimal who lived in France and told him what had happened. He said "enough is enough", he took a plane and came to the UK the next day.

He met up with my uncle and my cousin, and they all came to meet Rob's family in London with the hope to resolve the situation. I knew how aggressive and manipulative Rob and his family were. Since we would be in their house, I had to warn my brother not to be angry with what they said because I felt they would provoke him to be angry and use that to their advantage.

When we were at the house, Rob started shouting and screaming when he was complaining about me.

My uncle simply said to Rob "if you are screaming and shouting like this now, in front of us, how do you treat her when she is alone?"

That got Rob even angrier, then his sisters, his mother and father started taking turns in insulting my uncle and complaining about how I was not meeting the family expectations. They said that I was the reason that Rob was getting angry.

His father said, "a woman should work 27 hours out of 24 hours."

'I had heard this before, Rob speaks the same language as his parents'

Rob's father demanded that I pay more money because if they had to rent the house, they would have received more. My brother replied, "but she is not a tenant".

Rob, his mother and father, carried on insulting my family and were very rude to them. I remained quiet.

One of Rob's sisters sat behind me and kept on whispering in my ears, "you are lazy, you are lazy, you are lazy".

I realised that she was trying to provoke me to be angry so that they could react and accuse me of being the aggressive one. That did not happen; she didn't provoke me, she couldn't.

The family meeting was not going to end well. Therefore, we decided to leave, knowing there was absolutely no hope. I knew that too, but something inside me still did not want to give up. No one in my family is separated or divorced, so I never really thought this could happen to me.

My brother, my cousin and myself went back to the house where Rob and I live. None of my family members had earlier visited us in our home where Rob and I lived. They were not allowed to come over to the house before unless Rob's parents granted permission. For that reason, my brother stayed outside and waited for me to pack my bags. I brought my bags to the front door for my brother and cousin to take them to the car.

I took only my belongings and left everything that was gifted to me by them in the house. I made sure that I did not leave any mess and cleaned as I went.

When Rob and I got married, his family gave me some gold jewellery as part of our culture. I needed to make sure I returned them safely for my peace of mind. I did not want to take anything they gave me, and I wanted to make sure that the expensive jewellery gifted to me was returned to the parents safely.

I started to panic when I could not find the jewellery where they were usually kept. To my surprise, Rob had already taken them to his parents. My passport was also not in the drawer either. I remembered him dictating where I should keep my important documents and valuable things and insisted that they were kept where he had instructed.

I was stunned at how manipulative the situation was. I just wanted to make sure that they had the jewellery safely with them. I tried calling his parents' house, but they did not answer the phone. So, I walked to their house, but no one was home. That was the last time I stood in front of their door.

The first taste of freedom

It was time to leave; I had a leaden heart; although I felt I was being set free, I did not want to accept that I would have a broken marriage. I had tried to do everything I could to please, tolerate Rob and his family and try to make it work.

I could not believe that I was leaving. I felt relieved but at the same time very distressed and lost. My brother advised me that it was not safe for me to live independently yet, and it would be better to stay around family.

I was fortunate that my cousin Ravin and his beautiful wife Yogeeta supported me and welcomed me to stay at their house. They looked after me so well, were very patient and were very supportive. Having them around helped me feel very safe, loved and normal again. I could have open conversations with them, and they would advise me in my best interest.

Mindset matters.
mindset can break a mountain", that's how powerful the mind is!

Mindset can keep us from escaping any abuse. Many people think that it's just something they have to live with and carry on with life.

When we hurt any part of our body, we don't just live with the fracture, right? We fix it! It's the same for the mind. No matter how negatively an abuser has overwhelmed our views, opinions and desires, we have the power to fix it. It may take a while, but it is all fixable.

"If you can train your mind, you can also untrain it."

The hardest part for me was to accept that I was going through domestic violence and would be separated and divorced.

That's not how I had imagined my life, but asking for help meant that I had acknowledged what was happening, that it was wrong, and that I needed help to make a change.

I would not have been here writing this book today if I had not sought help.

Fear, anxiety, and lack of self-belief makes us feel like victims. Being around Rob and his family made me lose my self-worth, self-esteem, and confidence.

They made me feel so insecure, but in reality, they were the ones who were frightened and had insecurity within themselves. They also had some sense of helplessness.

Toxic people in our lives are weaker than us hence why they have to show dominance.

"All negative actions have a positive intention".
Jessen James Chinappan

That positive intention is for them, to help them feel better, to hide their weaknesses, fear and their self-belief.

The problem was never me!

Identifying Emotional abuse

Warning signs are challenging to identify in emotional abuse, so here is a quick overview of who the emotional abusers are. I have referred to them by specific names to keep up with the abuser's 'standards':

The Hypercritic: They constantly criticise to make you feel worse about yourself, feed on your insecurities to gain control and make you believe something that is not real.

The Scapegoat: An abuser will not take responsibility for their feelings, actions and life. They will completely deny that they had any part in the situation.

The Shamer: An abuser will constantly shame you, make you feel bad, say you have been an embarrassment, and use this to make you do what they like.

The Name-caller: A name-calling is a form of verbal abuse. An abuser will call you names that will impact you negatively.

The Punisher: An abuser will always find a way to punish you by hurting your feelings or using your weak points to threaten you.

The Coward: An abuser will convince you that no one else is there for you and that you should break your relationship with your loved ones. The abuser will have control over everything that you do and will want to isolate you.

Most emotional abuse will eventually turn into physical abuse, from grabbing your wrist to worse things. No matter what level of abuse it is, the impact is astronomical.

Mindset Strategy

The mind TLC

I am sure you are familiar with the term that we all need a bit of TLC in our lives. Here I do not mean "Tender Loving Care". Although we all need it, I refer to the mind TLC, "Talk Language Control", that can succour and maintain a robust and bulletproof mind. The mind TLC acts a shield to protect the mind.

Talk Therapy

> "The right people will catch you even before you fall."
>
> Harj Gahley

When was the last time you felt ashamed to talk about something?

Pain can start to heal when expressed. Wouldn't it be good if there was someone or someplace to turn to, even just for a quick chat or to ask for information without being judged or feeling ashamed?

There are many organisations for support in all areas of life and different types of problems. Many facilities are also available and provide facilities for confidential and anonymous calls to seek advice from professionals. Yet, some people find it hard to talk openly and run away from challenges instead of talking about them.

Sometimes when you go through difficult situations, it hurts like hell to talk and say how you feel. That's when you should share your feelings. Always speak to someone about your feelings and concerns with people you trust, strangers if need be, and if you connect, anyone you feel comfortable with, and professionals. These people do not have to be the only people you have known for a long time.

Everybody crosses your path for a reason and sometimes just when you need them to. It helps a lot to lean on people when you need advice and when you feel supported, you will gain courage, security, energy and hope. Speak openly and sincerely, and do not hesitate to go deep into the issue at hand.

My friend Harj Gahley whom I met through business training, is the founder of success unmasked, a successful and inspiring entrepreneur. He inspired me when he shared his story of a difficult phase in his life. He explained how he overcame feelings of loneliness, being lost and feeling weak through a system called the six principles of SHIELD.

This strategy will help you contact the right people to help you in the right way and help you turn to the right people at the right time. It does not necessarily mean you need to have many people, but it is all about having the right people.

The 6 principles of S.H.I.E.L.D

Support: Just because you have family, friends and colleagues in your life, it does not automatically mean that they are your support network. You may feel comfortable. Write down a list of people you feel comfortable with opening up to and who will be able to support you.

Honest: Being open and honest about why you are doing this encourages a sense of trust. Be honest with the outcome you want to achieve or the possibilities.

Introduce: Introduce yourself and build relationships with one another and support each other. People who know a bit of you will be more open to helping you. For example, you can say that you are struggling with your situation and you need support.

Energy: Building relationships takes time and energy but reaps tremendous benefits, positivity and support back. It may be tiring talking to different people and saying the same thing over again. Regardless, investing a little bit of energy in sharing your problems with other people will help you understand things from different perspectives.

Leverage: All individuals have different personalities. If you feel a certain way and do not have what it takes to deal with a problem, you can tap into someone else's ability to help you solve your problems. That will give you additional support in the right way, and some people can give you more logical aspects. Others will be able to comfort you. Leverage through people to help you manage your emotional state.

Dedication: When you have a support network, stay committed to seeking help and following up on your progress in dealing with your situation. If certain people are ready to give you their precious time, it's essential to take the opportunity of getting support. Become committed to achieving the outcome you desire.

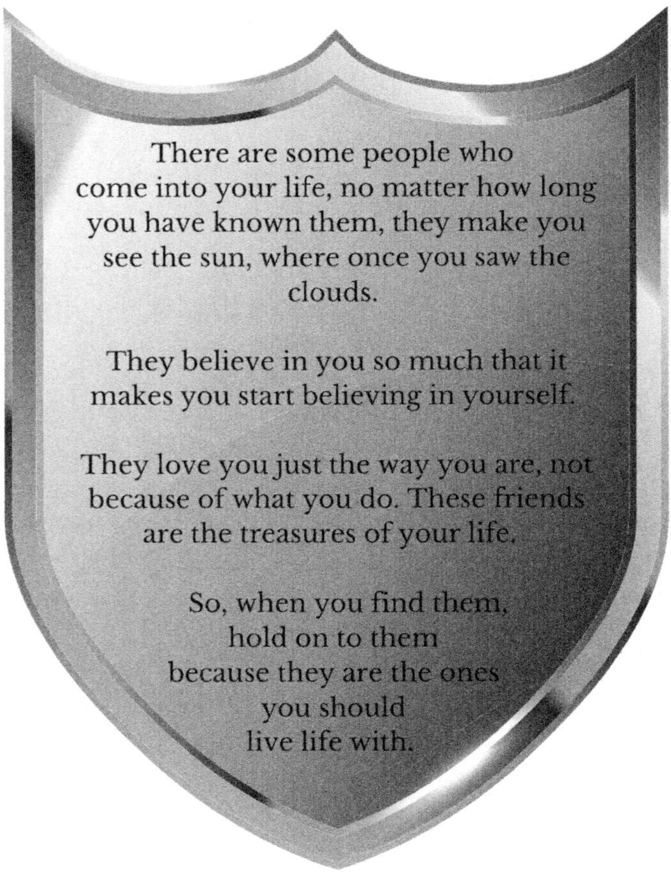

Language to self

> "Change your language, and you will change your thought."
>
> Karl Albrecht

Have you noticed that the voice in your head rarely stops?

Sometimes we are our hardest critic caster, which can be due to the language we constantly hear and fill our heads with. Our inner voice is affected by the language we use when we are talking out loud. We have the power to influence our inner voice and get it to be more supportive of us.

We have a conscious mind, a subconscious, and an unconscious mind. The conscious mind has immediate awareness of what we experience. It consists of things such as perceptions, memories, feelings and sensations. When I had to decide on whether to marry Rob, I had a strange feeling which I did not understand at the time. My conscious mind was telling me that I was overthinking things. I made the decision based on my observation rather than my innate feelings.

The subconscious mind holds information that is just below the surface of awareness. That's when we process what we hear and what we say. It believes everything we say, whether we say it out loud or in our head, true or not. The playground of my thoughts and feelings, my subconscious mind conflicted with my observations and conscious mind.

Then we have the unconscious mind made of thoughts and memories buried deep within ourselves, which we may not be aware of, but influence our behaviour significantly. It is like the inner voice calling from deep within, guiding us to make the right decisions. It is like you know something without knowing exactly how you know it. When I was dating Rob, my unconscious mind was telling me that there was something wrong. Like a wise man once mentioned, you can equate the unconscious mind with intuition; some call this gut feeling. My unconscious mind was giving me signs. I should not have ignored these signs that my intuition was giving me.

We should always listen to our gut feelings and never ignore our intuition.

However, we all make mistakes in life, but it does not mean that we have to punish ourselves with regretful memories. Some call it regrets, and some call it mistakes.

The past is the past, consider it as the rear view mirror in a car and keep on moving forward; away from it. There is no need to beat yourself up because of the past because it will cause negative thoughts, and language will impede your life ahead.

The negative language we hear or speak to ourselves impacts how we feel and behave, which can be detrimental to our self-belief and mindset. We need to be mindful of our thoughts and fight these negative languages to become stubbornly optimistic. Every time we negatively think about ourselves, we should immediately counter it with positive statements of power about ourselves. We can use this when someone else says something negative about us.

Affirmations help reprogram the subconscious mind to encourage us to do certain things and create the reality we want. The way it works is that the more an affirmation is repeated, the more it starts taking charge of our thoughts. Our thoughts are then going to change our feelings, and this, in turn, will change our behaviour. Ultimately this can change the decisions and actions we take.

Here are some exercises that you can do to help change your language to yourself:

The Mirror Exercise

Sometimes when we look at ourselves in the mirror we don't realise that we are talking to ourselves. Mirrors self-reflect deeper than you can imagine. It can evoke strong feelings within us; hence it can be an effective tool to help us change our perception.

The Mirror exercise is a very powerful tool. The mirror reflects beyond our true self; it reflects how we also feel and the areas that need change. If you want to have a happy and healthy life, then look at the mirror, look into your own eyes and say something positive. The most potent and quick way to get results is by affirmations to yourself. If you encounter that, it means you don't have what you desire and ask yourself 'why'. Look at the mirror again and say out loud, I am willing to change.

New beliefs will arise to the surface that has been causing you much trouble. Now think of where they came from? These are areas that you will need to change.

Sometimes, we all want our problems to be over, but we don't want to do the small things to help find a solution. We have the power within us that can transform every thought into an experience.

Only we have the responsibility to determine whether the experience will be positive or a negative one, and we have the power to change that. By acknowledging our responsibilities, we become more aware and learn to use this power consciously in a beneficial way.

Positive affirmation can release you from fear, negativity, anxiety and worry. Here are some examples:

Affirmation to yourself

I am worthy
I am much stronger than before because of the hard times I had.
I am wiser now because of all the mistakes I made.
I am happier now because I had painful experiences.
I am brave, bold and beautiful
I am proud of myself
I am enough
My pain made me powerful
My suffering gave me strength
My worries are now my wisdom
My fear gave me freedom

Control

> "If you cannot control your mind, your mind will control you."
>
> Ousha Demello

Life is life, and changes happen where you will find yourself in positive and hostile environments. When the negative situations turn into your hell, look out for the obstacles and setbacks as challenges you can meet rather than threats you want to avoid.

A strong mind will control your struggles to find possibilities, tackle more minor issues as soon as they arise, and make their way to an ideal situation. When you take control, you will feel empowered, giving you the ability to make better decisions.

There are many ways to empower yourself and influence all directions and outcomes in your life. Having control will give you a stronger mind, and a strong mind can shut out feelings of fear and inadequacy. Empty your mind of extraneous thoughts, and this will help you focus on the main problems. When the mind is quiet, that's the best time to change your mindset and the false belief you hold.

The power point is always the present moment. Sometimes, when we are in a difficult situation, we feel stuck or paralysed, preventing us from taking the right actions.

I want to remind you that you are never stuck.

You can make a change, and it starts right here in your mind. It does not matter how heavy the burden is, how long your problems and struggles have been with you. You can shift all of this today! Remember, you have power and authority over all your thoughts and actions.

Each moment gives you an opportunity for a new beginning, and the new beginning starts right NOW!

It's your world, your decision; you have the power to break any pattern and begin a new process.

Life gives you choices; if you want to settle for mediocrity in yourself, then that's what you will get, so don't be surprised if things do not go your way. Take control now because you are the one who can shape your destiny rather than just accepting events and situations as they come along.

Here are some examples of how you become more in control of your current situation and S.A.V.E yourself from misery:

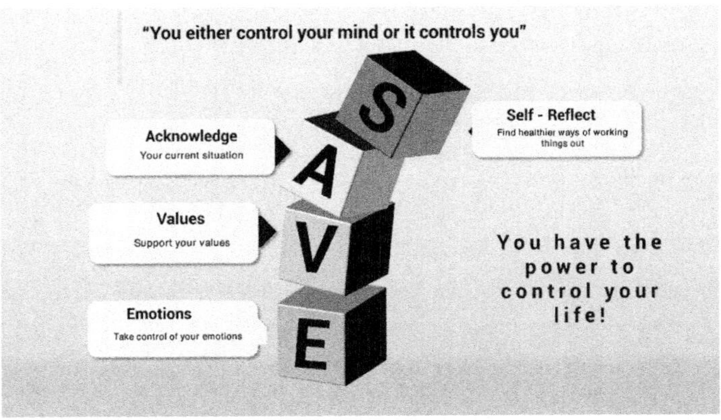

- **S**elf-Reflect: Accept yourself by knowing your strengths and limitations. Accept the good in you and embrace the bad, too, with the mindset to improve the things you struggle with.

  Self-reflection is a powerful, positive and healthy exercise and can turn your life around. Leaving yourself to feel guilty about something will only do more harm than good. When you self-reflect, you will be able to remind yourself that there are healthier ways of working things out.

- **A**cknowledge your current situation: You can start taking control by acknowledging your current situation, understanding what has been happening and determining what changes you would like in your life.

  Take control of your life and situation by accepting that you have to take the first step.

  Many people remain in a problem and wait for someone to come and rescue them. People are not going to be able to help you if you don't help yourself first. I know it is easier said than done, but taking that responsibility will put you in a better situation and have better control. If things do not go the way you expected, then what else could you do?

- **V**alues: Your values are the things that you believe are the most important in the way you live. Remind yourself of your values because this will help you get your priorities right and give you more control over your life. For example, what and who is important to you, happiness, freedom, stability, family, respect or money.

You can be content when things you do match your values and will give you satisfaction. However, when things don't align with your values, that's when things will start feeling wrong, causing unhappiness.

Whatever situation you may be in, you can control the direction of your life at any moment. Taking control of your life and living according to your actual values will become much easier to see what you should improve and change.

Now think about what you are doing that supports your values and how it is affecting your life. If you cannot determine your values, you can discuss this with someone you trust and who knows you.

Remember that your value doesn't decrease based on someone's ability to see your worth. Never devalue yourself because other people devalue you.

Sometimes just knowing your worth is enough.

You are enough!

- **E**motions: Our emotions are closely linked to our memory and values. When fundamental values are challenged, the feelings respond in a certain way. Understanding the link to memories and your values can help you control the emotional responses and allow you to overcome the challenges you go through and become more aware of your actions.

It is fundamental to express feelings in the right way. Expressing them improperly can make you lose control over the situation, harm yourself, worsen a situation or damage relationships even more.

Emotional decisions are made in the heat of the moment; hence emotions play a significant part in most of the decisions we make in life. Healthily respond to your feelings by breathing in and out for at least five seconds to help you calm your emotions down. As I mentioned earlier, speak out to people and write journals to help you better understand your feelings and identify patterns you would like to change.

CHAPTER 4

BELIEF

"Only make decisions
that support
your self-image,
self-esteem and
self- worth."

Oprah Winfrey

Back at the yellow line

Standing at the platform staring at the yellow line, deciding what to do next, would be the most critical moment of my life.

I was about to make a life-changing decision.

I wanted to jump in front of the train to end all the pain I was feeling. I was emotionally distressed, and I thought perhaps all my pain would disappear if I ended my life. I could not ascertain any other possibilities because Rob's voice tormented my mind.

I could not construct any logic or sense to make the right decision because my brain and memory became puzzled. I wanted him to understand that my life had a meaning, so I thought if I jumped in front of the train, he would then realise what he had been doing to me. All my focus was on how he was making me feel and how to make him understand that he was hurting me.

When I was staring at the yellow line waiting for the train to come, I suddenly saw my mum's face.

I thought to myself, 'oh my god, how will she feel if she sees me in pieces on the train track'.

> *'oh my god, how will she feel if she sees me in pieces on the train track'.*

Then I remembered my brothers and sisters who love me so much, who spent so much time, money, and effort making me the woman I am today. Then I saw so many other people's faces who love me.

At that moment, I realised that I would not make the pain go away by jumping in front of the train. I was going to pass it on to so many people who don't deserve it. Not for that loser!

I realised that the pain was not a problem. That pain was necessary to help me find my strength and to help me understand that I needed to make a change. I decided not to run away from my challenges anymore, but I would run *towards them* and *face* them.

I started to gain a bit more strength and felt I had more power because 'I have just beaten death, I can beat this situation, I will beat this, my life is not over yet, I have a family to live for'. As long as there is life in my body, I have to fight for it.

I realised that I could not control his behaviour, but I had the power to control my own life. I did not feel fear anymore because life is meant to be lived. I realised that fear and sadness have no place if I don't allow it in. I have the power to build a wall so that his voice cannot penetrate my mind. I cannot allow him or anyone to control my life and ruin it. He has no right to validate my purpose, destiny and certainly no right to take my joy away.

That pain is inevitable, but I felt empowered when I chose not to suffer anymore.

I chose to be bruised, not to be broken in pieces.

It was painful to consider that I would give up on life; this thought is as painful now as it was years ago. The difference now is that I should always listen to my voice and tap into my true self first. I now know that have the power to say this is NOT how the story my is going to end.

When I was staring at the yellow line on the train, I saw my mum's and siblings' faces, not knowing what to do. That allowed me to tap into the SELF-model I explained in chapter one. I went back to my past life, and that's what determined what future path I took. I got my self-belief back, and that saved my life.

***S**ELF - I tapped into my truth, what I was like before I met Rob, how I used to feel about myself, my life, my passion and my purpose, how people around me made me feel.*

***E**XPERIENCES - The memories of my wonderful childhood, loving experiences with my family, kindness, selflessness, patience, laughter, pure and unconditional love*

***L**ESSONS - How I was treated when things didn't go well, how much support and positive people I had around me, my ability to persevere*

***F**AILURES - the support and positive feedback I had when things did not go right. The situation I found myself in was in contrast to the morals with which I was brought up. My childhood was filled with pure unconditional love, laughter, happiness, goodness and protection. There was a* *morality of subtle submissions between people of goodwill and the people who wished me ill in my current situation.*

I could not get over the bitterness of what was happening to me. Anger and sadness were there because I bottled up anger and sadness for too long, which has turned inwards and, consequently, suppressed by self-belief. I was trying to fix what he said was wrong, but it was all a lie. He was a lie. The life I was living was a lie.

The problem was never me. There was nothing wrong with me. There was nothing wrong with the other two girls with whom the previous marriage was cancelled last minute either.

They both dodged the bullet. I didn't.

I fell into a psychological trap many people fall into.

I was being patient, loving, kind and tolerant to the wrong person.

The problem was him!

We cannot expect apples to grow on a Mango tree, it will simply never happen, and like an old saying, "a leopard cannot change its spots". Rob was a bully, an aggressive person, an abuser, manipulative and toxic.

These kinds of people feed on other people's insecurity to stop them from being themselves. Rob and his family are all control freaks, bullies, emotional manipulators and enjoy playing mind games.

Bullies are liars, weak and have insecurities, and that's why they become hurtful to others so that they can be seen as the powerful ones and take advantage of people's kindness.

Always remember that we are all humans at the end of the day. The only difference is our thoughts and attitudes, which can be changed. Unwanted behaviours can be eliminated.

Nothing I could have done would have solved the situation I was in. The only way was to remove me from it.

If you cannot remove a negative situation, remove yourself from it.

Every so often,
because of what we have been repeatedly told, it makes us have the same thoughts over and over again.

We don't realise that it is we who have the power to control those thoughts.

For example, we can refuse to think specific negative thoughts, just like we sometimes refuse to believe in positive thoughts to ourselves.

They have no power over us if we don't allow them in. Thoughts don't have meaning; they are just words strung together!

When these thoughts come, we have the power to define them into something nourishing and positive, and only we give them meaning.

When I was having suicidal thoughts, I was fortunate that my thoughts moved me back to my true SELF.

I remembered all the love my family had for me. I was able to thrust aside Rob's voice and listen to my power voice.

That allowed me to become stronger, tougher and more resilient.

I HAVE A CHOICE!

The BCD Life model

> "When you were born, you cried, and the world rejoiced. Live your life so that when you die, the world cries, and you rejoice."
>
> Cherokee

The BCD life model represents the cycle of life. There are two things that no one has control over on this earth, the day we are born, and the day we die. However, what happens in between is totally in our possession. We all choose what we do, how we behave, how we feel and how we want to perceive life.

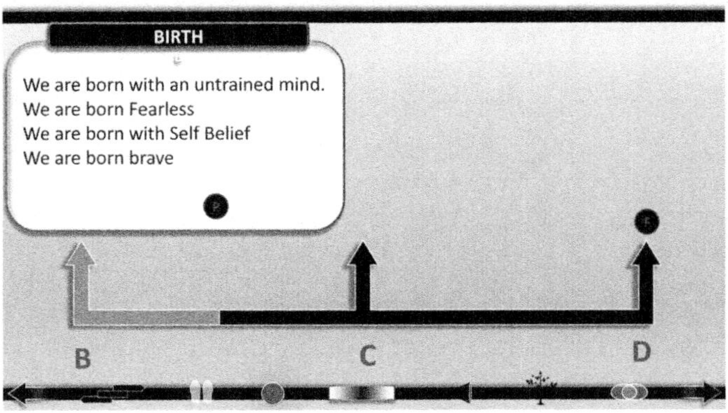

We are all born with an untrained mind, a mind that is fearless, brave and already has self-belief, ready to breathe and live. Different feelings come in the future because of the exciting and inevitable conflict between polarities of negative and the positive, between evil and good, between light and darkness, ups and downs, sadness and happiness.

As time goes by, we have to make decisions and assumptions about events that happen in our lives. Subsequently, we have different feelings such as sadness, feeling lost, confusion, depression, loneliness, change of mindset and impacting our self-belief because of certain things we perceive to be threats. These feelings create stiffness in our bodies and our mind. It makes us cling to old ways, making it difficult to see things outside the box, believing there is "no other way".

But life can be a simple process if we allow ourselves to see it that way. For example, when there is no light, darkness becomes automatic. When things are not correct, things are wrong; when goodness is not active, then bad moves in and if there is no success, there is a failure, and when there is no happiness, there is sadness.

I believe that our feelings are not based on reality at all. Our version of reality is built over time, and we make them our truth. By creating such beliefs, life seems to be a series of disappointments resulting in a feeling of hopelessness.

Hopelessness permeates the thoughts and the emotions, and it becomes easy to think that others are responsible for our problems and cannot resolve them. Many people tend to accept the dire situation they are in, thinking "it's life", or we must adapt, blaming ourselves for being in the situation or moving on without full closure.

When things do not work in our favour, it does not mean there is something wrong with us, nor does it lessen our self-worth. It's not what happened; it's how we react to it. We are responsible for all our experiences. Life is not bad unless we make it so unless we choose to look at it in that way.

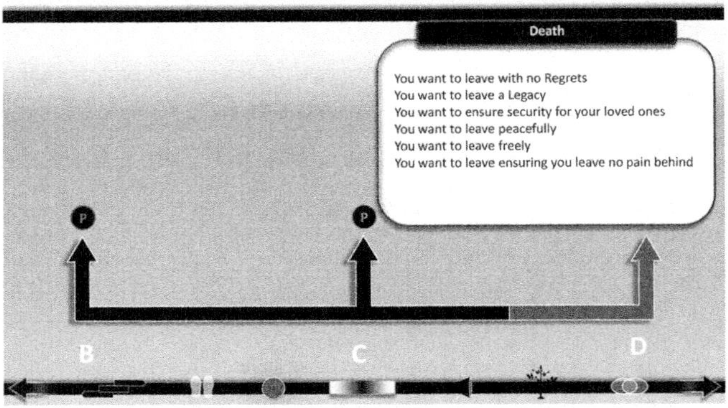

Sadly, the inevitable life cycle takes us to the stage where there will be a day when we will have to depart from the world. When the time arrives, we hope to be able to leave with no regrets, and we would like to leave a legacy and want people to remember us in a certain way. We want to make sure that our loved ones are secure, that we have not left any pain behind and that we can leave the world peacefully.

We are lucky to be in a world where we can choose and make things happen if we want to. No one is ever quite ready for this; however, to be able to leave properly, we need to ensure that we take the necessary actions. It may be more challenging for some than others. Nevertheless, knowing that this is an inevitable life cycle, it is fundamental that we do what is right while we are still living.

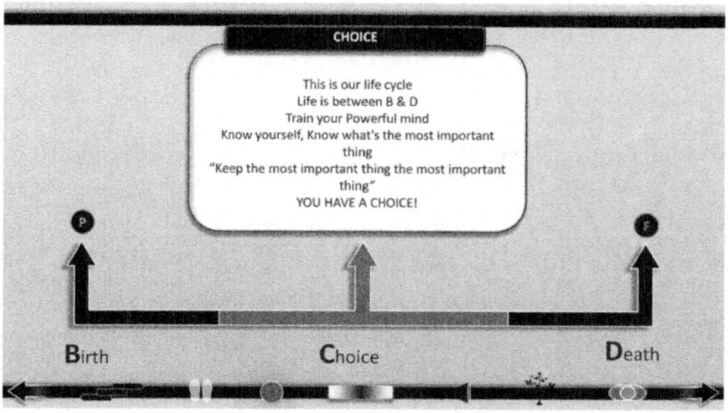

No matter what happens, we should never sweep our problems under the carpet. Instead we should understand them because it will help us rise above the situation and take control of our future. Avoiding a problem and wanting to give up will never make the pain go away.

When life gets tough, we might want to give up, and suicidal thoughts may creep into our minds, but we can come out of it and create a life where those thoughts have no place.

We are all blessed to have a choice, even if it is not apparent yet. We all can deal with any situation, and we do not have to deal with things independently.

When we cannot change a situation, we need to change how we deal with it. Many of us grow up with beliefs that become our resistance. In my case, I believed that 'I should not speak back even if I disagreed, 'I should be patient and tolerate people no matter if they are good or bad, 'I should be the one making more effort', 'we don't do divorce'.

These deep-rooted beliefs stand in our way of making desirable changes, therefore, hindering the path to a more fulfilled life. Surrendering to these changes facilitates the process of growth. We often hand over power and control to other people or situations and use this to justify resistance to change. These beliefs can cause delayed decision making, taking the right actions, and consequently living in denial of the need to change.

We have to embrace the life we want and take steps that will make it possible. The past cannot be changed, but our future can be shaped to how we want it to be.

JUST BELIEVE IN THE FIRST STEP.

> *"What we give out, we get back because the universe supports our belief."*
>
> Jessen James Chinnapan

If we choose to be helpless victims and believe that there is no hope, the universe will support us in that belief and trust me, there is only one way this can lead life to, and that is down the drain or, in my case, the train track. It is imperative to release the negative thoughts, ideas that do not support or nourish us.

The only things we are constantly dealing with are 'thoughts', which can be changed. Regardless of any problems, our experiences are just the outer effect of our internal thoughts. If we change them, the feeling will go, and hence we can make better decisions in life. We are responsible for our own lives; therefore, what happens externally is only a mirror of our internal thoughts.

I chose not to condone Rob's bad behaviour, but my belief that "whatever is happening is okay, it might be my fault" encouraged him to treat me that way. My thoughts permitted him to continue exhibiting his behaviour. Once the thoughts were gone, I was no longer able to endure them. You see, I broke that pattern.

Challenge the negative beliefs you hold about yourself and enlarge your territory because the universe will support your thoughts no matter what they are. Attitudes and beliefs are like weeds growing in the garden. Negativity is typical, it may not be beneficial, but it is normal. As much as we want to, we should not ignore it. We don't have to live in it, but instead, we should handle it as early as possible.

Loving and approving of yourself first, and creating a space of safety, trust, deserving and acceptance will create better thoughts in your mind, create better and more loving relationships and attract what you desire, whether it may be a better house, better job, better partner and even better you.

Once you are able to see your worth, you will no longer be able to tolerate people who don't.

Believing in yourself
should become a habit.

You become what you believe, and your behaviour will always follow your belief. Therefore, you should never let anything or anyone define you.

Only you have the right to define yourself based on the point of view that you care about.

Pain and struggling will teach you a lesson. This lesson will make you wiser; your wisdom will make you stronger, that strength will give you self-belief.

When you have self-belief, anything is possible.

You need to believe in yourself.

Sometimes we cannot take the correct actions because of belief. Hence, by changing the belief first, then changing our actions becomes easier.

How you feel will create thoughts, those thoughts will determine the actions you take. And the actions you take will define your path. Taking an action is a massive step; however, knowing the outcome you want to achieve first will conclude whether you are taking the right moves.

Here is a small but powerful exercise you can do to help you believe that you can make changes in your life if you want to. Let's consider the undesired feelings you have that you would like to change in the first column. In the third column are the desired (positive) feelings that you would like to feel.

Now think of the actions you will need to take to be able to change these feelings. Different situations will release other emotions and thoughts, so amend the desired feelings according to your problems.

No matter how you feel, your 'power' point is always in the present moment. So whatever situation you are in right now, take the right actions NOW.

Undesired Feelings	**What actions can you take NOW?**	**Desired feelings**
Victim		Victory
Fear		Fearless
Sad		Success
Angry		Affirm
Practice Stress		Practice Peace
Lost		Learn
Stuck		Support
Frustrated		Focus
Hate		Love
Giving up		Moving forward

CHAPTER 5

ACTIONS

"Whatever you do, do not run back to what broke you."

Frank Ocean

After leaving Rob's house, he tried to contact me through my mobile phone, but I refused to answer his calls. While I was at my new place of work one Monday, he suddenly appeared at the reception asking for me. When the receptionist told me his name, I felt my heart beating very fast and felt a bit of fear. I was hesitant; first, I did not feel like talking to him, but I thought perhaps I should hear what he had to say.

He tried to convince me to come back to his house. He told me that the house was not the same anymore; he was finding it difficult to live without me. I did not trust a word that came out of his mouth. When he realised that I was not falling for his lies, he tried something else. He knew that I love dogs, so he said he bought a dog, and I would love it.

He said that he knew this would make me happy hence why he got it. He had always been an excellent liar. Even though I knew he was lying in my heart, I felt that I needed to make sure. One of Rob's female neighbours, who was quite fond of me, kept in touch after I had left his house, and through a conversation with her, she confirmed there was no dog.

Rob had not changed. He was still very manipulative and a toxic liar.

On another occasion, he tried to convince me that we needed to have a baby so that mine and his family could start talking again. He said that was the only way to move forward. He carried on insisting on keeping in touch, constantly lying to me and wanting to meet up.

I played safe by talking to him on the phone instead of meeting up until I finally acknowledged that he had no good intentions. He just wanted to keep track of where I was and what I was doing.

He was still a control freak. He kept on messaging me, and I did not feel safe because I had a feeling he was up to something, perhaps trying to get back at me for leaving him.

He wanted to have control over me and my life again. Therefore, I decided to block him entirely on my mobile phone and social media.

> *The thought of him made me feel like I was in danger.*
> *I was certain that he would never be happy to see me move on or see me happy at all, definitely not after leaving him. I knew that he would prefer to see me dead than be happy without him.*

Soon after, I received a call from a random number. It was a guy called Raks who said he wanted to meet up with me. I felt this was a manipulative situation by Rob trying to lead me on to something. I just played along and pretended to be interested, but I never showed up where he wanted to meet. That was the end of it, so I guess he must have realised that I knew it was his doing all along.

Then, he started to use an impersonation of a female person named Christina on Facebook, started chatting to me online, and requested to become friends with some of my friends and family on Facebook.

Again, I sensed it was him. My suspicions were confirmed correct when the conversation became more and more aggressive. Christina told me, "you are going to die lonely. No one will ever want you. You have nothing". That was Rob's language. I immediately informed my friends and family, and Christina, aka Rob, was blocked immediately.

I realised that he would never leave me alone, and he would not rest his monstrous mind until something dreadful happened to me. Rob and his family were highly revolting people who would want to take revenge if things did not go the way they wanted.

Therefore, I went to the police station and applied for an injunction to keep him away from me. The injunction was served to him the same week. He did not adhere to the law twice and still made contact.

So, on both occasions, I reported him back. The police informed me that he was arrested and then bailed out. This time, reporting him to the police without hesitation seemed to have worked. He soon realised that he could not control me anymore and that there would be consequences if he tried.

Eventually, he stopped trying to contact me.

Forgiveness is a choice

"There are no justified resentments."

Wayne Dyer

Around a month later, I received a call from the police department asking me to file a harassment case against Rob and his family. I was not sure what to do as this had never really crossed my mind. I felt that I was fortunate enough not to be living in his house anymore, hence why I did not feel the need to do anything else.

I discussed it with my brother, who had helped me come out of the situation, he encouraged me to file the harassment case. I had his full support, and he soon started conducting some research and prepared a statement for me.

Nonetheless, I was not feeling content about it all. I did not feel comfortable punishing him and his family, even though they deserved it. I have never wished anyone anything terrible, and I did not think that punishing them would make me happy. I was already feeling at peace by being away from them and at that time, this was enough for me.

One Monday morning, while I made my way to work, I sat on a red bench at the bus station waiting for my bus to arrive when I suddenly saw a familiar face.

To my surprise, it was one of my good college friends, Erick, whom I had not seen for almost ten years.

We were both so happy to see each other. We exchanged numbers, and we met up a couple of times after, we chatted about the old days and our current lives. I was pleased to hear that he had married his girlfriend from college. When he heard about my disastrous marriage, he was shocked and angry.

I remember him saying, "I think we met after many years for a reason. I am now a newly qualified solicitor".

I was thrilled and proud of his achievements as he was a very hard-working student when we used to study together. I confided in him as a friend and not as a legal person, but he was very keen to support me and said he was happy to represent me.

Although the universe was opening doors for me, my heart wanted to forgive and move on.

I did not wish Rob and his family anything bad, and I did not want revenge or feel the need to have justice. I wanted to have a peaceful and happy life, and I had acquired a peaceful mind already by being away from their noxious environment. I could not imagine having to be around them again or dealing with them in any way at all. Although I knew I was in an excellent position to go ahead with the case because I had sufficient evidence, my mind and heart were constantly battling.

Moreover, I knew that if I filed a harassment case against Rob, his whole family would go down with him because they were also harassing me. Although they are all deserving of punishment, I did not have the heart to punish them. I have much compassion for older people. I strongly felt it would not give me any peace of mind by punishing him and causing grief to his parents or sisters.

Finally, I followed my gut intuition and heart, and subsequently, I informed my brother and friend Erick that I did not want to pursue the harassment case. I was sure that they were disappointed, but they respected my decision. Even though I was still sad about the whole situation, I had peace.

I started to appreciate life more, and I began to feel my true self again. That was enough for me. As time went by, I began to focus more on myself. I became a bit more spiritual; I kept in touch with my family and caught up with all my friends. I started to feel healed and felt a lot happier.

I found that forgiving gave me tremendous peace of mind. I chose to forgive but not forget.

Once we decide to forgive, the healing process will begin. Some of you may find it difficult to let go of negative thoughts and experiences or not know how to let go. Some choose to punish instead of forgiving.

Wanting to punish and seeking revenge is a natural thought when people hurt you, but the best revenge is to live your best life and show that no one can break you.

But firstly, it is crucial to understand that you are not your problem, and the problematic situations do not determine your worth and decisions.

By letting go and forgiving, you will become more solution-oriented than problem-oriented. It helps you gain control of the situation.

Not forgiving causes anger and resentment; it will keep you focused in the wrong place, which will cause more suffering for you. First start with forgiving yourself, then you will be able to forgive others, otherwise, you will give power away to the person who hurt you. When you are not forgiving, you are not harming the abuser; you are hurting yourself more.

If you find it difficult, you can try to set off some forgiving affirmations if you need to. For example:

My happiness does not depend on others

I stepped away from feeling Fear to feeling Free

I forgive those who hurt me. I can use that energy and pour it into my happiness.

I feel more peace and power when I forgive

The losers do not deserve my time, as my life is more precious than theirs

I feel free when I let go

Less baggage on my back helps me move faster

Let go

> "Moving on is painful, but staying stuck where you don't belong is even more painful."
>
> Sandra Ammerlaan

Letting go may not be an easy process for some. One of my good friends Sandra Ammerlaan is an NLP master practitioner, founder of laughatshit.com and a successful coach who shared some valuable tips on how you can let go of a belief, an experience, or someone. She said that letting go does not mean that you care less about them, but it means you care more. If you are in the position where you are holding on to something, it could be because of the picture you created around a situation, a person, or an experience.

You hold on because you want it to be different, but it is not, it is what it is, and that's the most arduous struggle. Sandra added that if you hold on, you are fighting with the situation, and as long as you are fighting with it, you cannot connect with it. When you hold on, you want to have control, consequently making you resentful from connecting.

Therefore, it is you who will end up getting hurt. The past situation is never going to change, but you can only let go.

Letting go of a connection, a person, or situation can have a hugely rewarding result in the longer term. Believe, trust the fall and let go.
It may not be easy immediately after letting go.
The fall may be uncertain, but the landing will feel good, and the onward journey will be rewarding.

John F.O'Mahony

Here are a few ways that can help you let go:

1. Cry it out

Letting go can still make you feel sad, guilty, or angry. Whatever feelings you may experience, don't bottle it up. These emotions must be released, and one way could be to cry them out. Crying does not make us vulnerable. Instead, it can help you and people around you to see your feelings and emotions in a way that no words can portray. Crying may be an excellent way to help you heal and restore your emotional equilibrium.

Most importantly, it will help you acknowledge the feelings you are experiencing and understand the situation better. When you cry, you clear old and toxic emotions you had and allow more room for new and better ones to come in; it is part of the process of letting go.

My good friend Dr Francis Ikhenemoh, a specialist in Mental health and author of the book Depression lies, also said that you should not forget that you are human. It is okay to melt down. Don't unpack and live there. Cry it out, and then refocus on where you are heading. Trust your intuition. You don't need to explain or justify your feelings to anyone.

Trust your inner guidance. It knows best!

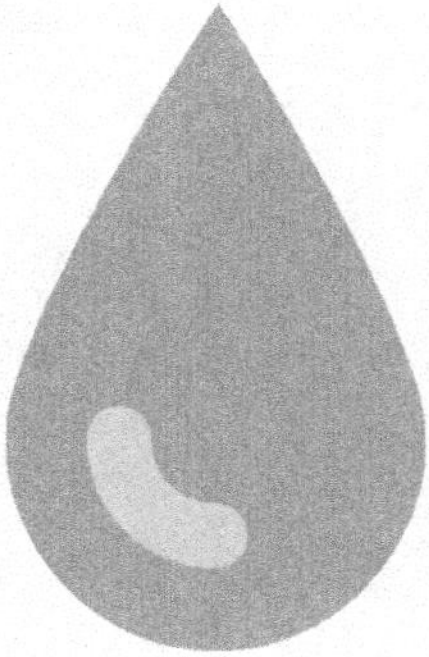

Crying are the words your heart speaks. Tears are the washing machine of your soul. It's a way of releasing what you need to let go of. It is not weakness, but strength to let go of what you've been holding on for too long.

Sandra Ammerlaan

2. Focus on the present

The 'power' point is always in the present moment.

Most of us tend to go through our days on autopilot, forming thoughts and judgements without conscious awareness of what we are doing. Not being in the moment disconnects from what is happening to our lives in the present moment, causing our minds to vault from thought to thought, making it harder to let go. Buddhists call them "monkey minds" because it is similar to a monkey swinging from tree to tree.

Whether by philosophers, Buddhist spiritualisation, or modern psychology, we have always been told that we should not worry about the past or the future and make the most of the present. Everyone I have spoken to also agrees that it is vital to living in the moment.

The question is, how?

You can start by focussing less on what is going on in your mind and more on your current situation. The mind overthinks, hence can blur the reality of what is happening. When the mind is clouded, false assumptions can cause impulsive reactions. False beliefs will impact your self-esteem, making it less likely to link your self-esteem to the situation, and you will be more likely to take things at face value.
Additionally, you will not judge yourself for how you feel. Instead, you will be able to acknowledge the thoughts you have, observe, note them, and it will

hugely benefit you to understand specific patterns. You could reflect on what makes you feel unhappy and what makes you feel happy.

When you acknowledge the current situations, it will help you practice mindfulness and allow you to reflect on your thoughts as they are. As a result, you will focus more on what makes you happy, enhance your self-esteem and help you take the right actions.

Focusing on the present moment will reboot your mind so that you can respond to your situation thoughtfully. For example, instead of being impulsive and reacting to the moment, you will accept the emotions you are feeling, and you will be asking yourself, "how do I respond to it?". Subsequently, you will have more control over your mind, behaviour, and actions you will take.

Focusing on the present is supposed to make you feel healthier and happier. If you find yourself not feeling good about your present moment, then that's a sign that you need to remove yourself from the situation and help you let go.

Some people I spoke to find it more challenging to focus on the present, feel anxious about their previous experience and future, and cannot focus on the present. If you think the same, then try these simple methods that I used and shared with others that have helped significantly in concentrating on the present moment:

- Take a minute and breathe. Breathe in and breathe out. Do it with your eyes closed and with an empty head if you can.

- Write your feelings in a journal. It is a good exercise that can help you set yourself in the right mind. You can do this anytime you feel comfortable too, but the most effective way of doing it is in the morning or the evening.

  You can do a visualisation exercise, visualise what kind of life you desire, and where are you at the moment. Realising that you are not living the life you were supposed to will help you tap into your current situation.

- Spend some time alone. Whether in a closed room or even better, a mindful walk alone will help you engage all your senses and step out of your current situation. Being alone will allow you to be able to connect with your authentic self.

3. Change your thoughts

When we face pain, our mind's natural tendency is to try and avoid it by resisting pleasant thoughts and feelings. But this will not make the thoughts go away. Accepting the unpleasant state will help you get certain things that are beyond your control. Situations can be beyond your control but not your thoughts.

Your thoughts impact your feelings, your feelings affect your behaviour, and your behaviour determines who you are. Remember that you are not your thoughts because you have the power to change them. You might feel you are still a victim even after moving away from a problematic situation, but you are not.

A simple strategy that helped me change my thoughts and advise others to do is instead of asking yourself the question "Why me?", change it to "why not me?".

When we go through a challenging situation, we may be tempted to ask ourselves why this happened to us? When you ask "why me", you are keeping yourself in the problem circle. You will give yourself all the reasons in the world why certain things happened. You then will wear the guilty hat, consequently making you more unhappy, stressed and angry.

On the other hand, if you ask yourself, "why not me" this will automatically give you all the reasons you should NOT be in the problem circle. Consequently, this will make you wear the problem solver hat.

Remember that you have already changed status simply by removing yourself from the problem itself. You are more than what you have become.

You are stronger than you think. You have the control of living your life in a way that will empower you.

You are fortunate to be able to find a new path in life that is best for you.

Take a moment to consider what your strengths and core values will help you seek out like-minded people that will help you live, grow and flourish following your true self.

Knowing your core values will make your life easier. It will give you a path to follow, understand your goals, and the aim to live a life you deserve. Hence this can support you in making it essential. For example, your core values could be love, dependency, honesty, happiness, or loyalty.

> "To make the best decisions, you need to ask yourself questions to check if your answers align with your core values. No matter what it is, your decisions must meet your core values, whether it may be independence, freedom, family, financial, stability, honesty, trust or integrity."
>
> Chloe Bisson

You could try this short exercise below to help you recognise your core values.

What are your Values	Why are they important?

Some people who have experienced past trauma or events such as breakups, domestic violence or other situations that have caused bad memories to imprint in their brain feel like it is impossible to move on. Some people always have the fear that past experiences they have been through might be repeated again. These thoughts can be rewired. Think of rewiring like reprogramming. You have the power to reprogram your thoughts.

Here are some ways of reprogramming your thoughts.

1. Trust – You may feel sceptical that things can change and that you will never get over the situation you are in. I get it; I have been there. You can start with the small part of you or the situation that you believe can change. To let go, you need to have faith and trust in yourself and life. Trust that you can take the right actions and make a change that will work best for you.

2. Accountability – Although your life or the situation you might be in seems to be out of your control, I can assure you that this is not the case. You are responsible for your own life, and you have complete control and power to make a change. You do not need others to give you closure unless to take responsibility for your own life. You are not alone; there is help out there. However, you have the first responsibility to have that control and clarity of what you want out of a situation, which will allow you to get the right people and support.

3. Disrupt the thoughts – Some traumatic circumstances can cause them to be so entrenched that some people find it difficult to change them. If you find it challenging to change your thoughts, you can disrupt them instead. You could start disrupting them by questioning them. Let's say if you are feeling like giving up on something, instead of thinking I am fed up, you could ask, "why am I fed up?"

These questions will automatically disrupt your thoughts and make you change them. Another way is to surround yourself with positive people. You can take on other people's energy without being aware of it, making you question your thoughts compared to others' positive thoughts.

Here is a quick example of how you can disrupt your thoughts:

Current thoughts	**Disruptive question**	**Answer the disruptive questions to change your thoughts?**
I tried my best	Is what I am trying worth it?	
It is my fault	What have I done that is right?	
I don't think I can get over this?	What haven't I tried yet?	
Why does this always happen to me?	Why shouldn't this happen to me?	

You are your priority.

> "Your past does not equate to your future, you have a choice to put all the crap behind and move on."
>
> Unknown

Even after coming out of my ruinous experiences and situations, they impacted my self-esteem, mental health, respect for myself, my lifestyle, mood, and happiness level. Although I was free and knew that I was in a better place, I was still emotionally unstable; I felt miserable and angry and frustrated with life because I knew that what had happened was not my fault.

I felt like Rob and his family did not give me a chance to show my worth. I did not have the strength or stamina to cope well with my new lifestyle, even if it was better than my previous life, simply because I felt I had lost my sense of identity. Although I had a brave face on and looked happy, my health and mindset were my last priority.

I still could not stop asking myself the same questions over and over again, "why did this happen to me?".

I remember having a conversation with my sweet mum, and she made me feel better when she said, "just forget about everything that happened, look at the situation as if you had a nightmare, now it is all over, pretend as if you didn't even get married, it was all in a bad dream. All you have to do now is to take care of yourself".

Her words made me feel better, and I started treating all the bad experiences with Rob and his family as if it was a bad dream. I slowly started to feel better and began to look after myself.

The first step towards my self-care was to protect my mindset through self-awareness of how bad things were for me and acknowledging that the changes that happened were necessary.

I started accepting that there was no weakness.

Instead, taking steps to change was commendable, and the outcome was positive. I started to believe in myself and started to make myself a priority.

Below is a simple method of getting yourself in the right mindset, making yourself a priority, ensuring that you have a healthier life, giving you energy, and giving you the strength to become the best version of yourself. It requires a small amount of TIME. Nevertheless, it is worth investing in because it is life's most wasted opportunity not being the best version of yourself.

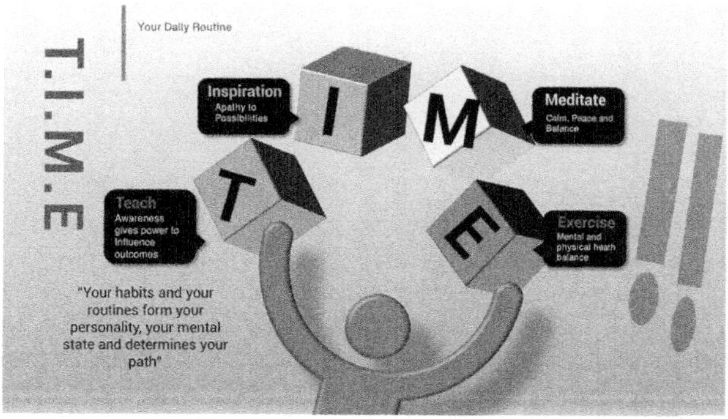

T.I.M.E

T – Train your brain every day.

Expand your knowledge by reading to enhance your awareness of how the mind works. Get others' points of view, talk and learn from the right people. If you are not comfortable talking to people from your surroundings, seek out help from professional organisations.

Teaching yourself is life's work.

The more you learn, the more you know, the more you believe and apply, the better you feel and the stronger you will get. In general, it is good to learn something new every day, which will help you use your memory more. You could do this by reading daily, even if it is just one page.

Reading and learning create awareness. It will help you become more informed of a different type of situation you may fall under to make the right changes, solve the problems and most importantly, acknowledge the issues you have that need resolving.

We are all born with a purpose; like Simba in the Lion King, his life journey deviated; however, he could regain his kingdom with the proper support. Read about previous similar cases, success stories and find out where to get help.

Associate yourself with positive and uplifting people you can learn from and who can support you in becoming the best version of yourself. You could also attend training or workshops to help you unveil your true potential and acknowledge your worth.

I feel blessed that I had the right support network. I educated myself about my situations, which helped me understand that I took the right actions, not having guilt, and finding closure.

Looking back and having gone through it all, the African proverb came to my mind "Smooth seas do not make skilful sailors". Sometimes we must face obstacles to learn and achieve goals. Remember that if the sea were always clear and calm, the sailor would never know how to handle a storm whenever you face a difficult time. Therefore, acknowledging mistakes and tackling challenges are all learning experiences that help us grow.

Your experience is your real teacher. You have learned a lot more than you can imagine, and it is time to become whom you are supposed to be. Keep on educating your mind, your heart and keep on evolving.

I – Inspiration

Emotional scars and hurtful feelings don't fade away quickly. For many people, the emotional impact may or may not fade away at all. Memories can cause upsetting emotions, anxiety, feeling numb, disconnected, unable to trust people again, and hopelessness on the brink of desperation. We tend to hide and run away from negative emotions.

Unfortunately, the more we avoid them, the stronger they get.

Although these are normal feelings and reactions to the abnormal situation you have been in, getting off this mind-numbing roller coaster of emotions and regaining happiness can be challenging, but it is not impossible. You may not like it, but the best way to deal with these emotions is to embrace them and try to befriend the negative emotion so that you can regain self-control again.

Recognising your current mindset and changing it will require some work. It is harder to do this alone, therefore join support groups that can help and support you wherever you are on your journey to inspire you from being a victor, not a victim.

Listen or read things that are inspirational to keep you in a positive mindset. When we are inspired, we can have a sense of purpose and boost positive motivations that will help us focus on the positive things, allowing us to take actions that will work towards our benefit.

Through inspiration, you can gain a better perspective of life, have more emotional stability, and provide a mindset shift. If you cannot change how you think about yourself, you can get inspired by how others overcome challenging situations. Staying inspired and motivated will help you find it easier to identify the benefits of making positive changes. It will also help you pick up the broken pieces and become more resilient, subsequently restoring your sense of wholeness.

Sometimes it can be hard to achieve things on your own, so you can get inspiration from people who have been in similar situations as you and who have overcome them, leading a better life today. There are many free support groups out there, whether they are face to face or online. You can do these by joining groups, communities, or even forming your own to either get inspiration or inspire others by sharing experiences. Other people's encouragement can significantly boost your motivation, particularly if you are facing more formidable challenges.

I was able to move on and feel optimistic about life because of the many people around me. My family and friends were highly supportive. I am now even more fortunate to have been surrounded by people who inspire me and encourage me every day. As a result of this and the ripple effect of my mentor and friends, I have built my community on Facebook, The Uplifted Mindset group, where I share inspirational speeches, tips on life and business.

Below is information from The Uplifted Mindset and other communities that I would highly recommend getting daily and weekly doses of motivation.

Ousha Demello: The Uplifted Mindset
https://www.facebook.com/groups/theupliftedmindset

Jessen James Chinnapan: Billion Lives Changed
https://www.facebook.com/groups/billionliveschanged

Dr. Francis Ikhenemoh: Mental Health Matters
https://www.facebook.com/groups/mentalthealthmatters.happinessdoctor

M – Meditate

Healing the mind is a little bit more complex than healing the body. Whatever the situation you may be in, the quickest way to stop feeling sorry for yourself is to create space in your life, build clarity and help you find a better perspective of life.

Meditation can be in any form, whether you actually perform meditation, praying or it could simply be spending some quiet time with yourself, with no disturbance, no people and no device. There is no right or wrong way to meditate as long as what you do is helping you shift into a positive and uplifting mindset.

Through meditation, in any way convenient to you, the mind can become more calm, peaceful and even better balanced. If you do daily meditation, you will be able to improve your memory, mood, attention span, and emotion and give you inner peace.

Even if it is only for five minutes, take a moment to breathe deeply. It will help you reframe negative thoughts that could stop you from making the right changes in your life. Our life is what our thoughts make it, so it is almost a must that you spend some time on it. When you meditate, it will allow you to check-in with yourself and find a deeper connection and a sense of purpose in life. It will also help you retake control and gain a new perspective on the situation and your life.

Through meditation, it will help you focus on the present, reduce negative emotions and will help you build the skills and courage to manage your feelings and situations better.

E – Exercise

There are plenty of reasons why you should exercise, not to mention the health benefits. Stress impacted me emotionally and also physically. I had lost quite a lot of weight, but exercising helped me physically and aided in relieving the stress and anxiety I was experiencing.

Exercise will get you in a better mood. People usually like exercising first thing in the morning because stretching the muscles and sweating can be a positive wake-up call for the mind and the body. By exercising, you will have more energy, much better attention, reduced stress and anxiety, which will resonate to a better mood.

Studies show that habitual exercise for about twenty to thirty minutes can improve your brain functions and memory long-term but most importantly, it will allow your mind to become calm. As well as toning your body, you will also be able to tone your thoughts positively.

All of the above will help your brain's plasticity, which is the ability of your brain to modify its connections and rewire itself. They will help you rewire your thoughts, feelings and hence improve your self-belief. Subsequently, this will boost your self-confidence overall, making you more aware of your physical and mental health.

Exercising will also help you with social interactions producing feel-good hormones, which will motivate you to spend time with family and friends or even grow your social circle.

Share your story

> "One day, you will tell your story of how you overcame what you went through, and it will be someone's survival guide."
>
> Haider Ali

Have you ever thought of sharing your story?

I grew up thinking that we should not be too open about our challenges because of fear of being judged, fear of being seen as weak, feeling ashamed, or even fear of being seen as stupid for being in a situation. I also had to consider how my story would make my loved ones feel, and I did not want to make them feel sad or angry. Hence, I never told them the whole story. However, whether they are good or bad experiences, we should not shy away from them because all these experiences determine who we are today.

Speaking out may not be something easy for some, it was not easy for me. I have achieved a lot of academic courses in my life, which allowed me to become an inspirational business trainer and mentor and gave me the knowledge and tools to help others start their businesses from scratch, but none of them taught me how to find my mighty voice.

I completed many other professional courses that allowed me to find my inner strength and tell my story in an empowered way. My previous experiences, academic and professional learnings and high-level mentorship have put me in a position where I can help and support other people to tell their stories to empower themselves and empower others. I now, also support women experiencing difficulties in life to enhance their branding, help them become an expert in their fields, and become more in control of their lives.

In this modern world, we are fortunate to have access to social media platforms where our messages and stories can reach thousands of people within a short period simply by doing a live recorded video or a post. There are also other powerful ways to share your stories, such as writing a book or an article. Some people find this challenging, but there are many ways to do it, whether paid to be done professionally or independently for free.

If social media and books seem too challenging, perhaps you can share with close friends and family. It will give you the opportunity for closure, as there is a saying that when we heal ourselves, we heal others too.

Although I managed to get out of my difficult situation within a year, it took me more than ten years to speak openly about it all. I first shared my story as a four-minute video and posted it on my personal Facebook page. I felt like I was ready. I felt empowered to do it as I have overcome the issues completely. I also thought that it was my responsibility to share to the world how I came out of such an abusive relationship with the hope that my message would serve someone out there who needs it.

After I posted the video, I was humbled by the responses; my inbox was inundated by heartfelt messages and voice notes by men and women thanking me for sharing my story and how I regained my power back. I was told that many people needed to hear the story and the message because it will give them hope and understand that they can overcome any situation they might be in if they believe they can.

It gave me more strength, knowing that my experiences are now for the world. I was humbled because when I shared my story for the first time on my personal Facebook page, people were not only keen to know more, but some also made contact asking me to support them.

Reflection

> "The stories we tell about ourselves reveal ourselves, construct ourselves and sustain ourselves through time."
>
> Kate McLean

How we talk about major events that happened in our lives has a significant influence on our personalities. Try to reflect on any bad situation that you have been in before. When you reflect upon this period of your life, you would probably perceive it simply as one of many episodes of events that were great but turned out to be damaging? Or do you see it as an experience that has toughened you up and helped you meet and appreciate people you have in your life today?

I used to kick myself for not writing this book earlier in life until I realised that it was not about telling my story that would shape my life and give me satisfaction. Instead, it was how I interpret my life now to tell my story that has impacted the kind of person I am today, resilient, powerful, confident, inspiring, and with a purpose.

We are all different, and we all self-define our stories. For instance, if you are the kind of person who would remember the positive things that came out of a bad episode, it is more likely that you will have a greater sense of well-being and satisfaction. The reason is that you will then allow yourself to acknowledge everything, digest, and reflect on what happened. Hence, it will enable you to explore areas you did not before to learn new lessons that can positively influence your life now and in the future.

Inspire

> "Sometimes, knowing that you are not alone in your struggles can be enough."
>
> Unknown

Life is truly a journey with inevitable ups and downs. Some experiences we have encountered may take longer than others. No matter what you had to face and what decisions or journeys you had to face, know that your experience and journey will inspire someone.

As mentioned in the last section, all your experiences, no matter how bad, played a part in shaping the person you are today. If you look back and see all the things you had to endure, they may have been hard to deal with, but they made you much stronger today.

You must have heard, "what does not kill you makes you stronger", you see, there is strength and power inside of you that you perhaps cannot see yet, but someone out there sees it and looks up to you and wants to be like you.

Your story is motivational to more people than you can imagine. You can bring strength to many people and motivate them to keep pushing and not to give up.

Through our stories, we share passions, joy, success, sadness, failures, fears, and hardships, which allow us to find common ground that helps us connect with people better.

Imagine a time when you struggled in your life and felt alone. How relieved and happy would you be if you knew someone out there had overcome the same problems you are facing, or even better if they shared how they overcame the issues?

Personalities like Tony Robbins, Oprah Winfrey, and so many others inspire and help millions of people worldwide and share things that you can't even imagine. They all had the same belief that if their story helps even just one person, it is already worth it.

Your life is an inspiration to someone, and you could even be the most impactful person in some stranger's life simply by sharing your story and your message.

Empower

"We all have the power to empower."
Corinna Stringer

No one likes to be exposed and often show people our most curated moments. However, we are always impressed with other people who open up about their struggles. We find them inspiring, brave and strong. We avoid vulnerability because we are afraid of what would happen if people know we are vulnerable when it comes to us. Our emotions arise from our core, and when we are feeling most vulnerable, we are more authentic, which empowers us to be our true selves.

Being vulnerable is more empowering because it will allow you to open your heart and be more self-accepting. After all, it will allow you to acknowledge that the feelings you experienced on an insecure journey were normal. Hence, it will enable you to become more capable of healing.

Vulnerability is not easy, but it can change your own life when you acknowledge what happened, and it can change many people's lives.

Vulnerability is not a weakness. Instead, it is a strength.

Being vulnerable will allow you to be your authentic self instead of pleasing others or fitting in. Hence it will help build better relationships with others and connect with people who will accept us for who we truly are. It will not only empower you, but it will also empower others to speak out too and know that there is a way out of any situation they might be in. You may not see it as such, but others see your vulnerability as courage, look up to you, are inspired by you and wish they could do the same.

Sharing your story can support a mindset shift; for example, you will stop treating yourself as a victim and choose to perceive yourself as a proud warrior who survived to inspire others. Owning the issues and showing the world how you overcame them will empower others to speak up. Let your mess become your message.

Your story matters, and there is much more power in sharing your stories than you think. Your rich experiences will help you understand your unique perspective, place, and purpose in this world.

You can transfer morals, messages, lessons, knowledge, strategies and most importantly, create more awareness. Share your story when you feel it's right and if you are still not above the situation, perhaps start with the SHIELD strategy in chapter 3.

STUCK

One of the most obvious questions that may come to people's minds who have not experienced abuse might be,

"Why don't people just leave an abusive relationship?"

Instead of blaming a person for staying in an abusive relationship, it is better to support and help them to leave. Leaving Rob was fortuitous as I was reactive to all his actions rather than proactively thinking of leaving him. It never even crossed my mind that I should leave, and this would have never happened if my brother did not step in.

Many other women are unfortunately still stuck in horrific situations, and because I have been there, I can understand why they don't simply leave. It is far more complicated than you can imagine.

Here are some reasons why people don't leave abusive relationships:

Self-worth – People in an emotionally abusive relationship may not understand that they suffer from abuse because there is no physical violence. Degrading treatments, insult, harassment, and name-calling makes people feel beaten down and of no value, consequently damaging their self-worth and left to feel like a shadow of their former self.

Victims may feel they will be alone forever if they leave or are scared of the possibility of picking another destructive relationship, hence staying hopeful that their situation will improve. Some people think that they don't deserve better, and as a result, this makes people feel there are no better options and no way to start afresh.

Thoughts – Being in an abusive relationship, being controlled and hurt is a traumatising experience and can cause distorted thoughts, leading to confusion, self-doubts, despair, guilt and even self-blame. Instead of leaving, one may feel like they need to help and save the relationship hoping that they can change.

They fear breaking up their family and believe that divorce or separation is not an option due to religious, personal or cultural reasons. There may also be fear of what other people will think. Abusers use gaslighting, explained in chapter three, to manipulate, emotionally blackmail and control their victims, preventing them from leaving.

Underestimation: A study by the Centre for Financial security found that 99% of domestic violence cases involved financial abuse. Abusers deliberately control a victim's finances to have power over their lives.

Financial limitations and no access to other resources make victims feel they have lost power, control their own lives, and are vulnerable. Consequently, feeling trapped in the relationship and making leaving even more challenging. Another reason is isolation, causing people to feel powerless hence underestimating any possibilities of leaving a relationship.

Children – Some women do not leave abusive relationships because of their children. They put their children first and sacrifice their safety. When Rob realised that I was not going to go back to him, he tried to convince me that having a baby was the right thing to do so we could start afresh and that the family would get along again.

I knew this was his way of getting me into a trap. Some people use children as a tool to get to their partners, but in the end, it is the children who get hurt.

Knave: There are many complex reasons why victims remain in abusive relationships. There is a cycle of abuse where a make-up honeymoon phase comes after an argument or an incident.

Knavish people can be very manipulative and would do or say something nice and, in some occasions, can also promise that they will never do it again. False hope can influence any kind and trustworthy person and therefore trust the abuser's words with the hope that things will get better, thus making it more emotionally difficult to leave. The more time spent with an abuser, the more control there is.

Domestic violence is all about power and control, and when a victim leaves the partner, that power and control that the abuser relishes are lost. Only the victim in a violent relationship will know the abuser best and understand the extent to which they can maintain control.

An abuser can be very unpredictable. More complex reasoning from the victim's view to stay in a toxic relationship is the fear of the repercussions of leaving the relationship. Research has shown that women are five hundred times more at risk of being harmed when they leave abusive relationships. Leaving a relationship can provoke violent responses.

Nonetheless, getting the right help and support can help leave a relationship safely, such as speaking to someone you can trust, your local authorities, and talking to the National Domestic Violence helpline.

It is also advisable to have a ready-to-go bag aside with essentials and essential documents if you need to leave in a hurry in case of any dangerous and unpredictable behaviour.

HELP

> "The best way to find yourself is to lose yourself in the service of others."
>
> Mahatma Gandhi

We all go through tough times. Some people going through some challenging phases in their lives may not know how to ask for help or may believe that it is okay to remain damaged in life circumstances. Therefore, if you suspect someone is struggling and going through a difficult situation, support them.

When I was at work, we were expecting a guest speaker to come to one of my lectures. At that time, I was still feeling trapped in the situation with Rob, and I had not opened up and spoken out yet. The guest speaker approached me and said, "You are going through some tough times, are you?" I didn't say anything. I didn't even know how and what to tell him he was there in such a short period.

I was so stressed, sad and anxious, that people started noticing it. Some people approached me, and some did not, simply because they did not know how to support me, not because they did not want to.

On other occasions, when I started speaking out, I was very fortunate to have people around me who wanted to support me. One of my work colleagues, a former Lecturer, Mr Harker, also approached me and kept on asking if I was okay. He had suspected that I was going through some tough times and gave me all the time I needed to talk to him. He was around sixty years old, and he said that his wife had been through the same situation as I am now, and she stayed in the relationship for 20 years, but I don't have to. He spoke to me every single working day and advised me in my best interest.

Whether it is a family member, friend or work colleague, there are many ways to support somebody you care about and empower them to make the best decisions for themselves while holding abusers solely responsible for their behaviour:

- **H**umble: Life is about helping and serving others. If everyone cared only about themselves, then we would get nowhere. Be available and willing to lend a helping hand wherever it is possible. Make uninterrupted time for the person you think might be struggling with, ensure that it is the right time to set aside sufficient time to listen in case the person decides to open up.

  Show empathy and agreeableness in allowing the person you are helping to know that you accept them for who they are without any judgement.

  People who choose not to speak out usually feel that they will not believe them if they tell others. For that reason, someone who knows the truth about their struggles can bring them a sense of hope and relief. You could assure the person that you believe in them, that it is not their fault and that they do not deserve this.

- **E**ngage: Like me, many people may want to avoid engaging in a conversation about the issues in their lives because they don't want to burden or stress other people about their problems. You could make the first move by tactfully opening a conversation. For example, you could say that you have noticed that... or you are worried about them. Some people may respond positively and say that they are fine and smile, but if you dig a bit deeper, you may find that their pillows are soaked in tears.

- **L**isten: If the person decides to open up, listen to their story without being judgemental. By listening actively, the person may tell you precisely what they need. Therefore, it is fundamental not to interrupt and listen before offering advice or suggesting solutions. If needed, ask more questions for further clarification, nevertheless allow the person to vent their feelings and fears because you may be the first person they open up to.

  It is imperative to validate the person's feelings even if you find them conflicting. For example, the person may express anger and guilt or love and fear. It will help to reassure the person that conflicting thoughts are normal, but violence is not okay. It is not normal to live in fear of being emotionally, financially or physically attacked.

- **P**roblematic signs: Some warning signs of abuse may be more transparent than others. Look out for the worrisome warning signs; for example, the most obvious are physical signs like sprained wrists, bruises around the arms or other parts of the body, black eyes, or busted lips.

You may also notice some troubling emotional signs can be fear, constant anxiousness, low self-esteem, suicidal talks or other symptoms of depression. People in a bad state will also have a change in behaviour such as becoming withdrawn, being late, isolating themselves from friends and family or cancelling appointments or meetups at the last minute.

Things that may seem obvious to you are entirely oblivious to the person you will support.
Some people may not realise their situation is abnormal because they have gradually become accustomed to the cycle of abuse and have no other models for their current relationship.

Therefore, as evident as it may be for you, it is essential to inform the person that abuse and violence are not part of a normal and healthy relationship and tell them that their situation can be dangerous and show concern for their safety. If needed, you may want to take necessary action in your own hands and inform someone who can support you further or the local authority if you feel the person is in danger.

A Final Thought

There is something highly therapeutic in writing my life events and emotions down. So much of the day is taken up with issues that need resolving immediately, leaving us limited space for reflection. Looking back, my heart is filled with gratitude to all the people who have helped me come out of my disastrous situation.

Life is like a marathon; the journey can be challenging, and obstacles can come in its way. However, you have the power to decide how you want your story to end at any moment. It will hurt when we are in a dark place, and it is acceptable not to feel okay, but it is not okay to remain in the dark and not do anything about it.

Like Les Brown once said, if we are too casual about things, we become a casualty. My mentor Jessen further elaborated this agreeing that failing, whether in a relationship or other areas of life, does not make you a failure. However, being casual could make you a casualty.

We have the power to choose whether we want to be bruised or broken in pieces.

Therefore, we should embrace the pain because pain is only temporary. That pain is going to become our power. Hence, we should never give up on ourselves, on hope and never give up on life.

Don't let people or any situation decide where we will end up, 'I am not supposed to end up in pieces on the train track'. It is whom we listen to, and every one of us should listen to our power voice because no matter what we are going through, there is a voice inside each of us that is stronger than anyone or anything around us.

Because I was able to change my belief, I felt much stronger. I decided to take control of the situation and face the consequences. I felt powerful, and my inner power voice was telling me:

"I am powerful because I stood up and asked for support

I am powerful because I chose to forgive

I am powerful

because

I LEFT IN PEACE,

NOT PIECES."

After I left Rob, I focused on myself, spending much time with my loved ones. I felt happier, free and peaceful. When I lived on my own, I felt connected, listened and trusted my inner self again.

Any accomplishments that have taken place over these years were the results of the love and support. I started meeting up with my friends and attending events. On one occasion, one of my good friends, Hagop invited me barbecue party at his house. During the party, I met some of Hagop's friends whom I had not met before.

That's when I first met Peter.

I felt connected with him straight away. We started chatting and exchanging contacts, we got along really well, and we have been inseparable ever since.

This time, I listened to my gut instinct.

I felt connected with my genuine intuition enabling me to make the right decisions, and I felt richly blessed to have been able to move forward together into a better future.

Your Power Voice

As a result of listening to my power voice, the man whom I used to call my husband is not my husband anymore.

In fact, I rebuilt my life with someone who celebrates me, not tolerates me, someone who sees the blessing in me and does not see me as a burden.

Now, I have a beautiful child and a beautiful future, and I did that because I listened to my power voice.

So, never give up on hope and never give up on life because there is a purpose for each of us; we need to give it a chance to be found in one piece, not in pieces.

Ousha Demello

Where To Get Help

https://www.womensaid.org.uk/
https://www.refuge.org.uk/
https://mensadviceline.org.uk/
https://galop.org.uk/domesticabuse/
National Domestic Violence Helpline **on 0808 2000 247**
Respect **on 0808 802 4040.**
https://www.nationalbullyinghelpline.co.uk/contact.html
0300 323 0169, 0845 225 5787
https://www.moneyhelper.org.uk **0800 011 3797**
https://www.nationaldahelpline.org.uk/**0808 2000 247**

The Author

Ousha Demello is an inspirational business trainer and mentor, and she has trained thousands of individual businesses over the last fifteen years. She is also an inspirational public speaker, Start up of the year 2021 award winner, most inspirational leader finalist, and the founder of the Uplift Academy. Ousha helps women start their businesses from scratch and scale their existing businesses so that they can have a less stressful life, spend more quality time with their loved ones, and work on their terms.

Ousha put her life's work, education, experience, and successful entrepreneurs' experience into creating a simple blueprint/road map called the UPLIFT blueprint to help those who would like to start and grow a business. The blueprint will help you no matter what stage of business entrepreneurship you may be in to create a successful and sustainable business and to scale it further.

She believes that women do not need to be empowered because women are powerful creatures already, but lack of clarity, guidance, distractions and prioritising other areas of life has stopped many women from achieving their goals and reaching their full potential. For this reason, Ousha also helps women unleash their inner powers to become an expert to have more time and more financial freedom.

Ousha Demello is the go-to person if you would like to have an uplifted mindset and to help you take control of your life.

Find out more at:

Website: www.ousha.co.uk
Facebook: **https://www.facebook.com/oushademello**
Instagram: **https://www.instagram.com/oushademello/**
LinkedIn: **http://www.linkedin.com/in/oushademello**
The Uplifted mindset group: **https://www.facebook.com/groups/theupliftedmindset**
https://www.flow.page/oushademello

Reference

Draghici, Alexander. "Post-Traumatic Growth: Can You Find Happiness after a Horrible Event?" *Happier Human*, 24 July 2019, https://www.happierhuman.com/post-traumatic-growth/.

Mitchell, Jerry. "Most Dangerous Time for Battered Women? When They Leave." *Ledger*, The Clarion-Ledger, 29 Jan. 2017, https://eu.clarionledger.com/story/news/2017/01/28/most-dangerous-time-for-battered-women-is-when-they-leave-jerry-mitchell/96955552/.

Robinson, Lawrence. "Emotional and Psychological Trauma." *HelpGuide.org*, 15 July 2021, https://www.helpguide.org/articles/ptsd-trauma/coping-with-emotional-and-psychological-trauma.htm.

Printed in Great Britain
by Amazon

72225862R00112